T0135481

A Framework for Automated HW/SW Co-Verification of SystemC Designs using Timed Automata

vorgelegt von
Diplom-Ingenieurin
Paula Herber

von der Fakultät IV – Elektrotechnik und Informatik
der Technischen Universität Berlin
zur Erlangung des akademischen Grades

Doktor der Ingenieurwissenschaften
– Dr.-Ing. –

genehmigte Dissertation

Promotionsausschuss:

Vorsitzender: Prof. Dr. Ben Juurlink
Berichtende: Prof. Dr. Sabine Glesner
Berichtender: Prof. Dr. Rolf Drechsler

Tag der wissenschaftlichen Aussprache: 25. Februar 2010

Berlin 2010
D 83

Bibliografische Information der Deutschen Nationalbibliothek

Die Deutsche Nationalbibliothek verzeichnet diese Publikation in der
Deutschen Nationalbibliografie; detaillierte bibliografische Daten sind
im Internet über http://dnb.d-nb.de abrufbar.

ISBN 978-3-8325-2511-8

Logos Verlag Berlin GmbH
Comeniushof, Gubener Str. 47,
10243 Berlin
Tel.: +49 (0)30 42 85 10 90
Fax: +49 (0)30 42 85 10 92
INTERNET: http://www.logos-verlag.de

Abstract

Embedded systems are usually composed of deeply integrated hardware and software components. They are often used in domains where a failure results in high financial losses or even in serious injury or death. As a consequence, it is indispensable to ensure the correctness of the digital components that control these systems with systematic and comprehensive verification techniques. To model and simulate complex HW/SW systems, the system level design language SystemC is widely used. However, the co-verification techniques used for SystemC are mostly ad-hoc and non-systematic. With that, it is either very expensive to verify a given design, or the results are not reliable.

In this thesis, we present an approach to overcome this problem by a systematic, comprehensive, and formally founded quality assurance process, which allows automated co-verification of digital HW/SW systems that are modeled in SystemC. The main idea is to apply model checking to verify that an abstract design meets a requirements specification and to generate conformance tests to check whether refined designs conform to this abstract design. With that, we obtain guarantees about the abstract design, which serves as a specification, and we can ensure the consistency of each refined design to that. The result is a HW/SW co-verification flow that supports the HW/SW co-development process continuously from abstract design down to the final implementation.

To establish a formal basis for our HW/SW co-verification approach, we define a formal semantics for SystemC. To this end, we present a mapping from SystemC to UPPAAL timed automata, which have a formally well-defined semantics. Using this mapping, we can automatically transform a given SystemC design into a semantically equivalent UPPAAL model. Furthermore, the resulting UPPAAL model allows the application of the UPPAAL model checker. With that, we can verify important properties of a SystemC design fully automatically, for example, liveness, safety, or the compliance with timing constraints. These properties are guaranteed for all possible input scenarios.

In addition to the formal semantics that allows model checking, we present a novel test algorithm for SystemC. The algorithm uses the UPPAAL model of a given high-level SystemC design to generate conformance tests for lower abstraction levels. Existing algorithms for the generation of conformance tests from timed automata models either support only deterministic subclasses of timed automata or compute expected results *online* during the test execution. The first is inacceptable because SystemC designs are inherently non-deterministic. The latter makes it impossible to reuse the conformance tests in multiple refinement steps. The algorithm presented in this thesis generates conformance tests *offline* and it can cope with *non-deterministic* systems. The result is a set of SystemC test benches that can be used to check automatically whether a refined design conforms to a given abstract design.

Together with our model checking approach for abstract SystemC designs, we obtain a framework for the automated HW/SW co-**Veri**fication of **S**ystemC designs using Timed **A**utomata (VeriSTA). The framework is fully automatically applicable and continuously supports the whole HW/SW co-design process. We implemented the complete VeriSTA framework and demonstrate its performance and its error detecting capability with experimental results.

Zusammenfassung

Eingebettete Systeme sind in der heutigen Welt allgegenwärtig. Sie werden zunehmend auch in Bereichen eingesetzt, in denen ein Fehler zu hohen finanziellen Verlusten oder sogar zu Verletzungen und Todesfällen führen kann, zum Beispiel im Automobilbereich. Als Folge davon wird es immer wichtiger, die Korrektheit eingebetteter Systeme mit systematischen und umfassenden Verifikationstechniken sicher zu stellen. Eine besondere Herausforderung ist dabei, dass in eingebetteten Systemen Hardware- und Software-Anteile eng miteinander verflochten sind. Um solche heterogenen Systeme zu modellieren und zu simulieren wird häufig die Systembeschreibungssprache SystemC eingesetzt. Die Verifikationstechniken, die für SystemC eingesetzt werden, sind jedoch überwiegend ad hoc und unsystematisch. Die Verifikation ist daher entweder sehr teuer oder die Ergebnisse sind nicht zuverlässig.

In dieser Arbeit stellen wir einen Ansatz zur Lösung dieses Problems vor. Wir präsentieren einen systematischen, umfassenden und formal fundierten Qualitätssicherungsprozess, der die HW/SW Co-Verifikation durchgängig über den gesamten Entwurfsprozess ermöglicht. Die übergeordnete Idee ist, eine Kombination von Model Checking und Konformitätstesten anzuwenden. Model Checking verwenden wir um zu zeigen, dass ein abstrakter Entwurf eine gegebene Anforderungsspezifikation erfüllt. Anschließend erzeugen wir Konformitätstests um zu prüfen, ob ein verfeinerter Entwurf konform zu diesem abstrakten Entwurf ist. Mit diesem Ansatz erhalten wir Garantien über bestimmte Eigenschaften des abstrakten Entwurfs und stellen gleichzeitig die Konsistenz verfeinerter Entwürfe über den Entwurfsablauf hinweg sicher. Das Ergebnis ist ein Qualitätssicherungsprozess, der den Entwicklungsprozess von der abstrakten Spezifikation bis zur finalen Implementierung unterstützt.

Um eine formale Basis für unseren Ansatz zu etablieren, definieren wir eine formale Semantik für SystemC. Zu diesem Zweck bilden wir die informell definierte Semantik von SystemC auf die formal wohl-definierte Semantik von UPPAAL Timed Automata ab. Basierend auf dieser Abbildung können wir einen gegebenen SystemC Entwurf automatisch in ein semantisch äquivalentes UPPAAL Modell transformieren. Dies ermöglicht auch die Anwendung des UPPAAL Model Checkers. Damit können wir wichtige Eigenschaften, zum Beispiel Lebendigkeit, Sicherheit oder die Einhaltung von Zeitschranken, vollautomatisch verifizieren. Neben dem Model Checking bildet die von uns definierte formale Semantik für SystemC auch eine Basis für Konformitätstests. Wir stellen einen Algorithmus vor, der aus einem abstrakten Modell alle möglichen (zeitbehafteten) Ausgaben berechnet und aus diesen automatisch SystemC Test Benches erzeugt. Diese können einen beliebigen verfeinerten Entwurf ausführen und automatisch prüfen, ob die Ausgaben dieses Entwurfs in der Spezifikation erlaubt sind oder nicht, also ob der verfeinerte Entwurf konform zum abstrakten Enwturf ist.

Mit der Kombination aus Model Checking und Konformitätstesten erhalten wir ein Framework für die automatisierte HW/SW Co-**Veri**fikation von SystemC Entwürfen mit Hilfe von **T**imed **A**utomata (VeriSTA). Das Framework ist voll-automatisch anwendbar und unterstützt den gesamten HW/SW Co-Design Prozess. Wir haben das VeriSTA Framework vollständig umgesetzt und demonstrieren seine Leistungsfähigkeit mit experimentellen Ergebnissen.

Danksagung

Die vorliegende Arbeit entstand während meiner Tätigkeit als wissenschaftliche Mitarbeiterin im Fachgebiet "Programmierung eingebetteter Systeme" unter der Leitung von Prof. Dr. Sabine Glesner. Bei ihr möchte ich mich ganz besonders bedanken. Sie hat mich immer aus vollem Herzen unterstützt und mir sehr viel beigebracht. Ohne sie wäre die Arbeit so nicht zustande gekommen. Ebenfalls sehr dankbar bin ich meinem Zweitgutachter Prof. Dr. Rolf Drechsler für seine freundliche Unterstützung, seine oft auch sehr kurzfristige Hilfe und seine wertvollen Anmerkungen.

Neben den Gutachtern gibt es noch zwei Personen, die ganz besonders zum Gelingen dieser Arbeit beigetragen haben: meine Kollegen und Freunde Lars Alvincz und Thomas Göthel. Ich danke euch sehr für all die inhaltlichen Diskussionen, wiederholtes Korrekturlesen und dass ihr immer für mich da wart. Ganz herzlich danke ich auch meinen Diplomanden Joachim Fellmuth, Florian Friedemann und Marcel Pockrandt, die sehr viel zur Umsetzung der Arbeit beigetragen haben. Allen meinen Kollegen möchte ich danken für viele hilfreiche Diskussionen und für die angenehme Atmosphäre in unserer Gruppe, in der man einfach gern zur Arbeit kommt und für alles einen Ansprechpartner findet.

Zuletzt möchte ich meiner Familie, all meinen Freunden und den Hausmädels für ihre Unterstützung danken, insbesondere meinem Freund Kaspar Scholemann und meinen Eltern, Hille Herber und Norbert Thiery-Herber. Es hat mir sehr geholfen, dass ihr mir immer zugehört und mir immer wieder gute Laune gemacht habt.

Contents

1 Introduction

Embedded systems are usually composed of deeply integrated hardware and software components, and they are developed under severe resource limitations and high quality requirements. In connection with the steadily increasing demands on multi-functioning and flexibility, the analog control components are more and more replaced by complex digital HW/SW systems. To meet the high quality standards and to satisfy the rising quantitative demands, the automatization of quality assurance processes for such systems is gaining more and more importance. A major challenge is to develop *automated* quality assurance techniques that can be used for the integrated verification of complex digital HW/SW systems.

1.1 Problem

SystemC [IEE05] is a *system level design language* that supports design space exploration and performance evaluation efficiently throughout the whole design process even for large and complex HW/SW systems, and thus it is widely used in HW/SW co-design. SystemC allows the description of both hardware and software, and the designs are executable on different levels of abstraction. As a consequence, *co-simulation*, i.e., the simultaneous execution of hardware and software, can be used for validation and verification throughout the whole design process. For quality assurance, however, simulation is necessary but not sufficient. This has three reasons: First, simulation is incomplete. It can neither be applied to all possible input scenarios (in particular for real-time and non-terminating systems), nor can it be assured that all possible executions are covered in the case of non-deterministic systems. Second, although HW/SW co-designs are developed in a refinement process where an abstract design is stepwise refined to the final implementation, it is very difficult to ensure consistency between different abstraction levels, or to reuse verification results in later development stages. Third, simulation alone is not sufficient for a systematic and comprehensive quality assurance approach because the degree of automation is limited. The evaluation of simulation results has to be done manually by the designer, e.g., by inserting assertions about the expected behavior all over the design.

1.2 Objectives

The aim of this thesis is to establish a framework for the automated HW/SW co-verification of SystemC designs. We require the framework to fulfill the following criteria:

1. The proposed co-verification techniques must be suitable for both hardware and software parts of a given digital control system, and they have to be able to cope with the main co-design concepts, namely concurrency, time, reactivity, hierarchical modeling and abstract communication. Due to the implementation of concurrency in the SystemC scheduler, this includes the requirement to support non-deterministic system designs.

2. The quality assurance process should be comprehensive and *continuous*, i.e., it should support the complete system design flow from an abstract design down to the final implementation. In particular, we want to ensure consistency between different abstraction levels in a refinement process and to reuse verification results from high abstraction levels on lower abstraction levels.

3. We require the co-verification techniques used in the proposed framework to be automatically applicable and efficient. To give evidence for that, the framework should be completely implemented. It should be applied to case studies that demonstrate its efficiency in terms of performance and of error detecting capability.

A vital precondition for automated verification techniques is a formal semantics for SystemC. This is due to the fact that automated verification techniques require a clear and unique understanding of how to interpret a given design or model. Unfortunately, the semantics of SystemC is only defined *informally* in [IEE05]. As a consequence, we derive as a subgoal that we have to address the problem of defining a formal semantics for SystemC. We require our formal semantics to fulfill the following criteria:

(i) The behavioral semantics of SystemC informally defined in [IEE05] must be completely preserved.

(ii) To maintain comprehensibility, the structure of a given SystemC design has to be preserved.

(iii) We want the formal model of a given SystemC design to be generated automatically.

(iv) The formal semantics must be suitable for automated verification.

(v) For debugging purposes, there should be tool support to edit, visualize and simulate the formal model of a given SystemC design.

1.3 Proposed Solution

To achieve the objectives defined above, we propose a quality assurance process based on a combination of model checking and conformance testing. We assume that the HW/SW co-design process starts with an abstract design that is stepwise refined down to the final implementation. We propose to use model checking to verify that the abstract design meets its requirements, and to generate conformance tests to verify that refined models or the final implementation conform to the abstract model. This approach yields a formally founded and comprehensive assurance process that

- continuously supports the HW/SW co-design flow throughout the whole design process,

- ensures consistency between different development stages,

- allows reusing verification results and

- has the potential to be fully automatically applicable.

Model checking is an automatic verification technique. With model checking, it can be proven that a model of a finite-state concurrent system (described by a system specification) fulfills certain requirements. In contrast to simulation or testing, model checking is *complete*, i. e., it covers all possible input scenarios and all possible execution paths. With that, it is possible to *guarantee* important properties such as liveness, safety and compliance with timing constraints. The precondition for the application of model checking is a formal model of the specification. In our approach, the specification is given as an abstract SystemC design, whose semantics is only informally defined.

To obtain a formal semantics for SystemC designs, as required for the automatization of verification techniques, we propose to map the semantics of SystemC to the formally well-defined semantics of UPPAAL timed automata [BLL⁺95]. Using this mapping, we present an approach to automatically translate a given SystemC design into a semantically equivalent UPPAAL model. This allows the application of the UPPAAL model checker to verify safety, liveness and timing properties. Furthermore, UPPAAL timed automata have the expressiveness to represent most of the SystemC language constructs and execution semantics. The only exceptions are dynamic process and object creation and the restriction that only bounded integer data variables are used. As we will see, these are minor restrictions. More important is that interactions between parallel processes, including dynamic sensitivity and timing behavior, can be naturally modeled. Compared to other state based modeling languages, UPPAAL is especially well-suited to model and to verify timing behavior. This is vital because system designs often contain synchronous hardware and asynchronous software. In both the SystemC design and the UPPAAL model, systems are regarded as networks of communicating processes. In our transformation approach, we map SystemC processes to UPPAAL processes. The execution of these processes is controlled by a timed automaton that models the SystemC scheduler. We use parameterized timed automata for events and for primitive channels. The timed automata modeling SystemC processes, events, channels and the scheduler are synchronized by UPPAAL channels. All automata that are necessary to represent a given design are generated separately and composed into a system using the UPPAAL template mechanism. This makes the generation process highly scalable and the generated UPPAAL model compact, comprehensible, and flexible towards design evolution. To ensure the correctness of the transformation, we first ensure that the transformation of SystemC processes into timed automata processes preserves their informally defined behavior. Second, we ensure that the semantics of interactions between processes is preserved. The resulting transformation from SystemC to UPPAAL preserves the informally defined semantics of SystemC and the structure of a given design, can be applied fully automatically, and yields direct access to the UPPAAL model checker.

The aim of conformance testing is to determine whether an implementation of a system conforms to its specification. To this end, it is necessary to define the notion of *conformance* precisely. In formal testing theory, this is defined by a formal *implementation relation*. Widely used and well-established in the context of model-based testing of labeled transition systems is the *input output conformance* (ioco) relation introduced by Tretmans [Tre96]. Based on the *ioco* relation it is possible to evaluate test results automatically by comparing the outputs of the implementation with those of the specification. If the implementation sends an output that is not foreseen by the specification, the test verdict is *fail*. If the implementation sends all expected outputs for a given input trace, the test verdict is *pass*. The automatic generation of conformance tests based on the *ioco* relation consists of the computation of all possible outputs of the specification for a given input trace. The resulting set of expected output traces can then be used as a *test oracle*. This allows the automated evaluation of test executions by comparing the output traces produced by the implementation with the expected ones.

The main challenge in the generation of conformance tests for SystemC designs is that they are inherently non-deterministic due to the semantics of the SystemC scheduler defined in [IEE05]. Furthermore, SystemC designs are usually developed in several refinement steps. Thus, it is desirable to have test cases that can be applied repeatedly in each refinement step. As a consequence, we require our conformance test generation approach to meet two important requirements: First, it should be applicable to non-deterministic systems, and second, the expected simulation or test results should be computed *offline*, such that they can be easily reused in later development stages. To generate conformance tests under these requirements, we first use our mapping from SystemC to UPPAAL to translate an abstract SystemC design into a semantically equivalent UPPAAL model. Then, we use the UPPAAL model to statically compute all possible output traces for a given test suite consisting of a set of input traces. When the test suite is executed on a refined design or on the final implementation, we can compare the output traces produced by the refined design with the output traces computed from the UPPAAL model of the abstract design. To decide whether the refined design conforms to the abstract design, we use the *relativized timed input/output conformance (rtioco) relation* presented by Larsen et al. [LMN05]. Based on that, we can use the output traces from the UPPAAL model as a *test oracle* to test the conformance of the refined designs to the abstract design fully automatically.

1.4 Motivation

Embedded systems are ubiquitous in today's everyday life. They help us making breakfast, buying a ticket at the ticket machine, and provide daily entertainment with radios, DVD players, TVs and video games. However, these applications are only the tip of the iceberg. On top of that, we also confide our lives to embedded systems which control our cars, trains and airplanes, traffic lights, and medical equipment. The latter class of embedded systems is a particularly severe challenge for their engineers, as they move between the conflicting priorities of safety, performance, and resource requirements. A field where those conflicting priorities are extremely hard to reconcile is the automotive sector. Automotive systems are safety-critical, as their failure may result in death or serious injury, the resource limitations are rigorous due to large quantities of production and the high cost pressure. At the same time, the quantity of digital hardware and software is heavily increasing, and already accounts for up to 30% of the overall cost of a car [Bro05].

To achieve design solutions with maximal performance at minimal cost, it is indispensable to explore the whole design space. In an application area where hardware and software persistently interact with each other and are to a great extent interchangeable, this requires an integrated design methodology. The demand for such an integrated design methodology has led to the idea of HW/SW co-design. In HW/SW co-design, a detailed high-level description of the complete behavior is made prior to design selection and HW/SW partitioning. This behavioral description then serves as an input to an optimization procedure that uses performance estimations to select the overall design and partitioning. This allows the evaluation of different design alternatives, and at the same time leads to an early consideration of HW/SW interfaces and thereby eases system integration. While co-design techniques have become comparatively mature, not least due to the development of powerful languages for the design of digital HW/SW systems such as SystemC and SystemVerilog, co-verification techniques still lack to keep pace with the advancements. In particular, the degree of automatization of co-verification techniques is limited. Although co-designs have become executable on different abstraction levels, and co-simulation is extensively used in every design stage, simulation results are still evaluated manually or semi-automatically by inserting assertions about the expected behavior all over the design. Although the concept of HW/SW co-design requires a behavioral abstract description of the system that serves as a specification for the following refinement steps, this description is still not used to automatically assure quality and conformance of subsequently developed designs. On top of that, the techniques to ensure the quality of the behavioral description are also premature and insufficiently automated, at least in case of a timed description. Together, this makes HW/SW co-verification an expensive, time-consuming, and error-prone task.

With this thesis, we contribute to this field with a framework for automated HW/SW co-verification of digital SystemC designs. Our approach allows both the automated verification of a given high-level design as well as the automated evaluation of the conformance of refined designs to the abstract design throughout the whole design process. SystemC became our language of choice because it permits to use a single language for specification, architectural analysis, test benches, and behavioral design. SystemC provides all of the substantial concepts of HW/SW co-design languages, such as concurrency simulation based on delta-cycles, time, reactivity, hierarchical modeling and abstract communication. With a solution that can cope with all of this, we are confident that our approach can also be transferred to other co-design languages (such as SystemVerilog).

1.5 Research Area

The issue of HW/SW co-verification establishes a point of intersection of many research areas. HW/SW co-design taken by itself is already an interdisciplinary field, which brings together the hardware world and the software world, communication and network experts, mechatronics and control engineers, and many others. HW/SW co-verification adds the dimension of topics connected with quality assurance. Analysis techniques, formal verification, testing and simulation can all be made applicable to co-verification with appropriate adaptations. Furthermore, the very different techniques from the area of hardware verification have to be combined with those from the area of software verification. For this thesis, the main research areas in which it is embedded are HW/SW co-design, formal verification, and testing. With respect to HW/SW co-design, we use current research results from system level design, transaction level modeling, and HW/SW co-simulation. With respect to formal verification, the relevant research fields can be narrowed to model checking, formal specification and semantic-preserving transformations. In the field of testing, our work can be classified as research belonging to the areas of conformance testing, in particular input/output conformance testing, black-box testing, real-time testing, and automated test generation.

1.6 Main Contributions

The main contributions of this thesis are:

- A **formally founded and comprehensive HW/SW co-verification process** for digital HW/SW systems modeled in SystemC, which continuously supports the HW/SW co-design flow throughout the whole design process. The proposed process is based on a combination of model checking and conformance testing, ensures consistency between different development stages, allows reusing verification results and is fully automatable. We published this approach in [HFG09, Her10].

- A **formal semantics for SystemC** that is defined by a mapping from SystemC to UPPAAL timed automata. This allows the application of the UPPAAL model checker to verify that an abstract SystemC design meets its requirements. In particular, a given SystemC design can be automatically translated into a semantically equivalent UPPAAL timed automata model. This exempts the designer from the time-consuming and error-prone task of developing a formal specification manually. We published this approach for model checking SystemC designs in [HFG08].

- An **algorithm for offline conformance test generation** for SystemC designs. The algorithm uses a UPPAAL model, which was automatically generated from a high-level SystemC design, to compute all possible output traces. SystemC designs are non-deterministic. We mitigate the state space explosion problem by exploiting specifics of the SystemC semantics to drastically reduce the number of states that have to be kept in memory. From the resulting output traces, we generate SystemC test benches that evaluate the conformance of a given low-level design fully automatically. We published the basic algorithm in [HFG09].

- A *Framework for Automated HW/SW Co-**Verification** of **S**ystemC designs using **T**imed **A**utomata* (**VeriSTA**), which shows the applicability of our approach. With an Anti-Slip Regulation and Anti-lock Braking System (ABS/ASR) as case study, we demonstrate that the complete framework can be applied fully automatically to digital HW/SW systems. Using the ABS/ASR example, we furthermore demonstrate both the efficiency and error detecting capability of our framework.

1.7 Outline

This thesis is structured as follows: In Chapter 2, we give an introduction to HW/SW co-design and co-verification, to model checking and conformance testing, and to SystemC and UPPAAL. Then, in Chapter 3, we review related work on HW/SW co-verification, in particular approaches that target SystemC, and related work on conformance testing for timed systems, in particular for UPPAAL. In Chapter 4, we present our approach for a comprehensive and continuous quality assurance of digital SystemC designs. The proposed quality assurance process is based on a combination of model checking and testing. In Chapter 5, we present our approach to transform a given SystemC design into a semantically equivalent UPPAAL model, which can then be verified using the UPPAAL model checker. In Chapter 6, we present our approach for automated conformance test generation and conformance evaluation for SystemC designs. To show the practical applicability of our approach, we have implemented the complete VeriSTA framework and applied it to three case studies. In particular, we use an Anti-Slip Regulation and Anti-lock Braking System to demonstrate both the performance of the framework and its error detecting capability. The main characteristics of the implementation are summarized in Chapter 7. The experimental results are presented in Chapter 8. We conclude in Chapter 9 and give an outlook on further research topics.

2 Background

In this chapter, we give a brief introduction to the main topics that are connected to this thesis. First, we introduce the concepts of HW/SW co-design. To this end, we describe the HW/SW co-design flow and the idea of *transaction level modeling*. Second, we identify the main challenges in HW/SW co-verification and review common co-verification practice. Then, we give a general overview over verification and validation techniques and define some important terms we use in this thesis. We also introduce the verification techniques that are most relevant for our approach, namely model checking and conformance testing. Finally, we introduce the two languages that are in the center of our approach for automated HW/SW co-verification, i. e., the system level design language SystemC and the formal modeling language UPPAAL timed automata.

2.1 HW/SW Co-Design

Embedded systems are usually composed of deeply integrated hardware and software components. In some systems the hardware part is fixed, but the increasing demands on performance and quality requires more and more that the hardware fulfills very special requirements and that it is precisely adjusted to the embedded software. As a consequence, it is often no longer sufficient to use prefabricated hardware components. When dedicated hardware has to be developed for an embedded system, the development of the embedded software depends on the progress in hardware development. The classical design flow for such hardware/software systems is shown in Figure 2.1. It starts with an abstract specification, e. g., the algorithm or another functional description of the desired system behavior. The specification is then partitioned into hardware and software modules. The decision which parts of the systems should be implemented in hardware and which in software is often guided by experience. For example, in video processing applications, the transformation of single frames (e. g., redundancy reduction and quantization) must be performed in high-speed and is usually implemented in hardware, while the composition of the frames is usually done in software. After the HW/SW partitioning, the design flow diverges and hardware and software parts of the system are de-

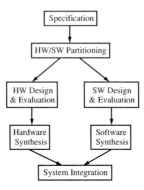

Figure 2.1: Classical Design Flow

veloped separately and independently. The integration of the hardware and software modules is not done until the last development step.

The separation of hardware and software design flows severely increases the system integration effort and makes it difficult and error-prone. For example, if the HW/SW interface definitions show deficits or if the communication between hardware and software designers is insufficient, system integration requires a lot of debugging and re-design. Furthermore, the later defects are revealed, the more expensive is their removal. If they were injected in early development phases, the designers often have to go back through the complete design cycle to detect and to mend them. Besides the cost and quality issues, a major drawback of the separated development of hardware and software is the issue of performance. The early HW/SW partitioning does not allow the evaluation of different design alternatives, and thus sacrifices significant optimization potential. HW/SW co-design is an approach to overcome these problems.

2.1.1 Design Flow

The idea of HW/SW co-design came up in the early 1990s [PP92, EHB93, GM93, KL93]. The central point is that hardware and software are developed together in an integrated system design process. The resulting co-design flow is shown in Figure 2.2. As before, it starts with an abstract specification, but now, the HW/SW partitioning is not fixed at the beginning. Instead, it is part of an iterative process, where different design alternatives are evaluated and compared. As a consequence, it is possible to explore the whole design space and to find an optimal HW/SW architecture. Furthermore, it allows an early analysis of HW/SW interfaces and thus reduces the cost of integration and defect removal.

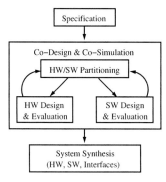

Figure 2.2: HW/SW Co-Design Flow

An essential component of co-design methods is HW/SW co-simulation, which is necessary to evaluate and compare different design alternatives. In a HW/SW co-simulation, hardware and software parts of a system are simulated together. For example, an Instruction Set Simulator (ISS) is executed together with a VHDL (VHSIC[1] Hardware Description Language) module. This provides an integrated way to simulate the interactions between hardware and software. At the same time, it allows performance evaluation if performance parameters like the delay of each module and the timing relations among events are simulated.[2]

The main challenge in HW/SW co-simulation is that hardware and software designers talk in different languages. They use different abstraction levels, different models of computation, different programming languages and different tools. These differences make it complicated to bring the design processes together and to unify them in a single co-simulation framework. To promote unifying frameworks, it is vital to gain insights into the relationship between different models of computations [Lee02]. An important question is how to combine synchronous and parallel hardware modules with asynchronous and sequential software models correctly and efficiently. As the software is finally executed on hardware, a simple approach to maintain correctness is to simulate both hardware and software on the lowest level of abstraction, on register transfer level. This is a feasible solution, but it exhibits the drawback of very slow simulation speed. In particular, if the processor design and the compiler are not part of the optimization target, but merely input parameters, the low-level simulation produces a huge unnecessary overhead. To solve this problem, there exist two (complementary) approaches: multi-level simulation and transaction-level modeling. Multi-level simulation means that modules on different abstraction levels are simulated together. Transaction level modeling

---

[1]VHSIC was a 1980s U.S. government program to develop very-high-speed integrated circuits.

[2]Other performance parameters could be for example energy consumption, memory usage, and space requirements.

tries to subsume hardware and software modeling under a common model of computation. At the same time, it provides abstractions that are suitable to speed up simulation without sacrificing correctness. The transaction level modeling design methodology can be easily extended to include multi-level simulations. In the following, we briefly introduce the principles of transaction level modeling.

2.1.2 Transaction Level Modeling

Transaction level modeling (TLM) [Ghe05, Kli05, CG03] was introduced by Synopsis around 2000.[3] The general idea of TLM is the rigorous separation of *computation* and *communication*. A system is regarded as a set of communicating processes, which can be structured in modules. The processes model functional processing units, i. e., the computations. The communication architecture is modeled by channels, which interconnect processes and modules. Data exchange is modeled by *transactions*. The concept of transactions is the heart of the TLM approach. A transaction is an abstraction of any possible information exchange between processes. For example, a transaction could represent the exchange of an abstract data type, but also of a concrete signal on a physical wire. At the same time, the processes can also be modeled on different abstraction levels. As a consequence, the transaction model can be instantiated with different models of computation. For example, a data flow model could be instantiated by using purely functional processes and FIFO (*first in first out*) channels for the exchange of abstract data types. At the lowest level, a *register transfer level* (RTL) model could be instantiated by modeling combinational circuits as processes and data exchange with registers.

To obtain a systematic design methodology, TLM defines a set of abstraction levels, which guide the way through the stepwise refinement process from an abstract behavioral specification down to the final implementation. The abstraction levels can be classified according to their modeling accuracy. The dimensions of modeling accuracy can in turn be divided into *functional accuracy* and *timing accuracy*.

The TLM design flow used in HW/SW co-design is depicted in Figure 2.3. Figure 2.3(a) illustrates the structural view, where emphasis is put on the architecture definition, Figure 2.3(b) illustrates the behavioral view, where emphasis is on the behavioral refinement, e. g., data and time refinements. Both views are conceptually different, but complementary in the design process, as a structural refinement always refines the behavior and vice versa.

Both from a structural and a behavioral view, the first step is to derive a *functional model* from the system specification. To this end, algorithms and functions are selected that are suitable to implement the purpose of the system. This model is used to define and to validate the functionality of the system. As

---

[3]The term transaction *level* modeling is a little bit misleading because TLM is not a single *level*, but a modeling technique covering different levels of abstraction.

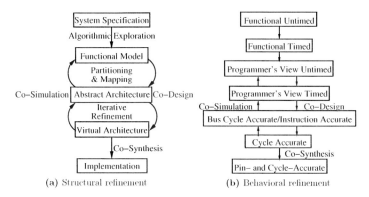

(a) Structural refinement   (b) Behavioral refinement

Figure 2.3: TLM Refinement Flow

time plays an important role in nearly all kinds of embedded systems, the first step after defining and validating the functionality of a system is usually to add approximate timing information to processes and channels. This yields a first impression about the timing behavior. To that end, from a behavioral view, an *untimed functional* and a *timed functional* model are distinguished. In this early design phase, time is usually over-approximated because an important goal is to assess the feasibility of the design and to get preliminary performance estimations. The resulting timing constraints on processes and channels can be regarded as time budgets for later design phases because they constitute the upper bounds that must be obeyed to meet the system timing requirements.

When the functional model of the design is validated and the preliminary performance estimation turns out to be satisfactory, the next step is to map it to an *abstract architecture*. To this end, the functional model is partitioned and mapped to abstract hardware and software components. From a behavioral view, this mapping is the transition to the *programmer's view*. Now it is possible to add more realistic timing information, depending on the HW/SW partitioning. Still, the timing information is over-approximated, such that timing constraints can be interpreted as time budgets for later design phases.

In the next design phase, the *abstract architecture* is mapped to a *virtual architecture*. To this end, each partition (or component) is either refined manually or existing modules (*Intellectual Properties*, IPs) are used as implementation. The manual refinement includes refinement of the data granularity and timing behavior. On the software side, the modules are implemented in a high-level programming language, and real-time operating system functionality is added where necessary. The compilation of the software components yields an *instruction accurate* model. On the hardware side, communication channels and protocols are chosen, and hardware data types are defined. This yields a *bus cycle accurate* model (e.g., a VHDL design). From the *bus cycle/instruc-*

tion accurate model, a *cycle-accurate* model can be derived. The result of the iterative refinement phase is a cycle-accurate, synthesizable system design.

In the last step, the final *implementation* is synthesized, which is *pin-* and *cycle-accurate*. This is usually done automatically by *electronic design automation* (EDA) tools.

2.2 HW/SW Co-Verification

In the last decade, embedded systems have become omnipresent in everyday lives. At the same time, they are increasingly used in cost-critical and life-critical applications, for example in the automotive sector or in the medical sector. This has led to a drastically heightened significance of design correctness of these systems. Unfortunately, conventional verification and validation techniques are difficult to use for quality assurance of embedded systems. Harris [Har05] attributes this to the high complexity of these systems, which stems from their size and their heterogenity. The considered systems are timed and have to meet strict real-time requirements. They often consist of a large set of concurrent or parallel processes exhibiting non-deterministic behavior. A particular problem is the composition of synchronous and asynchronous subsystems. Last but not least, verification techniques are usually designed either for hardware or for software, and conveying them to the other is not trivial. Nonetheless, several co-verification techniques evolved over the last few years.

In general, one can distinguish between formal co-verification as a static and complete technique, and simulation and testing as dynamic and incomplete techniques. Formal co-verification approaches either use abstract formal specifications which are suited for the description of both hardware and software parts of a system, such as finite state-machines (e. g., [BCG+97, Lee03]), or they try to combine formal verification methods for hardware and software, e. g., bounded model checking and inductive proofs [GKD06]. Most of these approaches focus on functional verification and do not consider non-functional properties such as real-time behavior. However, exactly those properties gain more and more importance in recent developments, in particular in the embedded system domain. Naturally, non-functional properties such as the abidance of real-time constraints and dependability are vital in safety-critical embedded systems. As it is difficult to formally verify non-functional properties, simulation and testing are more popular in the HW/SW co-design and co-verification community. Following Harris [Har05], simulation and testing for HW/SW co-verification involves three major steps:

(i) input selection

(ii) co-simulation or test execution

(iii) evaluation of simulation or test results

The co-simulation or test execution involves the common execution of hardware and software components and their interactions. Typically, a *test bench*

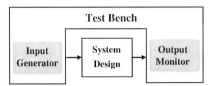

Figure 2.4: Structure of a Test Bench

is used to provide the system with inputs and to observe its outputs. To this end, it usually consists of an *input generator* and an *output monitor* as shown in Figure 2.4. The aim of automatic test generation techniques for HW/SW co-simulation is the automatic construction of test benches, i.e., the construction of input generators and output monitors. Ideally, the output monitor does not only observe the outputs, but also evaluates their validity. In the following, we discuss input selection, co-simulation and the evaluation of simulation results in more detail.

2.2.1 Input Selection

An important task to make co-simulation systematic and to allow automatization is *input selection*. The term *input selection* denotes the selection of inputs from the set of possible inputs. This includes the selection of input events, the determination of points in time where they should be sent to the design under test, and test data generation. Together, these constitute an input trace. In case of embedded systems, the real inputs are later provided by a technical environment. In general, the number of possibilities to provide an embedded system with inputs is infinite. This has several reasons: first, as these systems are often non-terminating, the length of an input trace is generally infinite. Second, as these systems are timed, and time is real-valued, their exists an infinite set of possibilities at which points of time inputs could be send. Third, also the input data may be real-valued and thus infinite. The infinity of input scenarios makes *exhaustive* or *complete* simulation and testing generally impossible. Thus, *input selection* is a vital task for simulation and testing of embedded systems.

In the co-simulation setting, the environment is replaced by a test bench, which provides inputs and observes outputs. In our context, the test bench can be regarded as an *environment model*. In this terminology, one can distinguish *open environments*, which may provide arbitrary inputs at arbitrary times (e.g., randomized), and *restricted environments*, which only provide inputs at certain times, orders and ranges. It is important to note that knowledge about the environment can be used to limit the number of test scenarios, and to concentrate on possible or likely inputs. Of course, for robustness or fault tolerance testing, an open environment model is preferable.

Regardless of whether a test bench corresponds to an open or to a closed environment, there exist different strategies to select simulation or test inputs from the infinite set of possible inputs. The basis for assessing the quality of a given set of inputs (i. e., a test suite), and thus for the selection of a "good" test suite, is a *fault model*. A fault model allows the concise representation of the set of all possible design errors of a given system. With that, the *coverage* of a test suite with respect to a given design can be evaluated. For example, a popular fault model in the software domain is *statement coverage*, where a potential fault is associated with each line of code. Using this fault model, the coverage of a given test suite with respect to a given design can be evaluated by computing the ratio of statements executed by the test suite to all the statements in the design. Other typical fault models from the software domain are control- and data flow based like *branch coverage*, *path coverage* or *domain coverage*. In the HW/SW co-design domain, state machine based fault models like *state coverage* or *transition coverage* are widely used. In the hardware domain, the most popular fault models are *stuck-at coverage* and *toggle coverage*. In general, one can distinguish randomized, coverage-directed, and fault-directed input selection.

For *randomized input selection*, test inputs are chosen randomly. At arbitrary times, a random event is taken from the set of input events, and test data is generated randomly. It is also possible to define probability distributions for input events and test data. To determine the delays between input events, it is reasonable to use exponential distributions. Randomized input selection allows the fast generation of large test suites, but no conclusions about how much of the design is tested can be drawn.

For *coverage-directed input selection*, the test generation technique heuristically modifies an existing test suite and evaluates fault coverage to decide whether the modification yields an advantage. A popular technique for coverage-directed input selection is the use of genetic algorithms together with a cost function which is used to evaluate new test sequences. It is also possible to use randomized input selection together with a cost function to achieve a certain coverage. Coverage-directed input selection is potentially less time-consuming than fault-directed techniques because efficient heuristics may be used to modify the test suite. However, the quality of the resulting test suite depends on the used heuristics.

For *fault-directed input selection*, the test generation technique targets a specific fault and constructs a test sequence to detect that fault, e. g., using path conditions. The resulting fault coverage is evaluated to decide whether the test generation process should be terminated. Popular techniques for fault-directed input selection are constraint solving at constraint and data flow graph (CDFG) level for software, and BDD based techniques such as *satisfiability* (SAT) solving for hardware. Fault-directed input selection allows the systematic derivation of minimal test suites with maximal coverage, but can be very costly in terms of computation time.

2.2.2 Co-Simulation

In HW/SW co-simulation, the design under test, including hardware and software components, is executed in a simulator. Conventionally, there is a gap between the simulation techniques used for hardware and those used for software. Typically, hardware is simulated by event-driven simulators with picosecond accuracy, e. g., on register-transfer level or on gate level. Opposed to that, software 'simulation' is usually performed by simply executing the code, possibly together with a *real-time operating system* (RTOS), on any processor which supports the RTOS and the interpreter of the language [Har05]. Co-simulation techniques often bridge the gap between hardware and software simulation by explicitly modeling the target processor, by compiling the software for it, and by simulating the execution of the software on the processor model together with the hardware components. An alternative to that is the approach of executable system-level design languages such as SystemC or SystemVerilog. There, hardware and software tasks are modeled in a common language and run concurrently in the simulation. The expressiveness of these languages also allows the explicit modeling of hardware/software interfaces and interactions.

The challenge of co-simulation is to be *efficient* and *accurate* at the same time. These goals contradict each other. In general, a higher accuracy always leads to lower performance. Thus, it is vital for co-simulation techniques to choose the appropriate abstraction level. As we have seen in Section 2.1, the TLM refinement flow defines a set of abstraction levels with ascending accuracy. On the functional level, no data or timing details are modeled. As a consequence, functional models can be executed with very high simulation speed. At the further end, pin- and cycle-accurate models contain all data and timing details needed for hardware and software synthesis. These models can only be executed with very low simulation speed. The models in between, e. g., bus-cycle and instruction accurate models, are often referred to as *transaction level models*. They are part of the TLM design paradigm, i. e., details of communication among computation components are separated from the details of computation components. For co-simulation, it is important that unnecessary details of communication and computation are hidden in a transaction level model and may be added later. As a consequence, transaction level models speed up simulation drastically opposed to commonly used hardware models such as RTL models. At the same time, they allow the evaluation and validation of design alternatives in HW/SW co-design at a high level of abstraction.

2.2.3 Evaluation of Simulation Results

The aim of the evaluation of simulation or test results is to inspect simulation or test traces in order to decide whether the system behaved correctly for a specific input trace, or whether a defect was detected. One possibility to achieve this is to inspect simulation or test traces manually. In most cases, this is not only error-prone but also unacceptably time-consuming. A prerequisite for the automated evaluation of simulation results is a machine-readable description of the expected or correct system behavior. To that end, it is necessary to formalize the expected behavior somehow. For that, there exist two complementary approaches: *assertion-based* and *specification-based techniques*.

Assertion-based techniques require the definition of a set of *assertions*, which are dynamically checked during simulation or test execution. Assertion-based techniques are particularly well-suited for validation purposes, because system requirements can often be directly formalized as a set of assertions. In addition, assertions are generally well-suited to formalize plausibility checks, e. g., on variables representing physical data. A great advantage of assertion-based techniques is that they can be directly derived from the requirements, and no formal model of the system is required. A major drawback is that the assertions that can be derived from the requirements are usually coarse-grained. Manual effort is necessary to translate them into machine-checkable assertions that are related to the concrete signals of the final implementation. Furthermore, the assertions have to be inserted manually.

Specification-based techniques are based on a formal model, which is used as specification of the expected or correct system behavior. The evaluation of simulation results is done by comparing the behavior of the system implementation with the behavior of the formal specification. A specification-based technique which is broadly elaborated in the literature is *conformance testing*, introduced by Tretmans [Tre96]. There, a *conformance relation* is used to decide whether the implementation conforms to the specification. There are two major advantages of conformance testing: first, if an executable formal specification is available, conformance testing can be applied fully automatically. Second, conformance testing is especially well-suited to ensure consistency when a design is refined from specification to implementation, as it is for example the case in model-driven development processes or in the typical HW/SW co-design flow.

Overall, assertion-based and specification-based techniques for the evaluation of simulation or test results are complementary and should be used together. Assertion-based testing is especially well-suited to check whether a system fulfills the requirements, specification-based testing is better suited to ensure consistency between different models in a model-centric design flow. As conformance testing plays a major role in this thesis, we give a more detailed introduction to that in Section 2.3.3.

2.3 Verification and Validation Techniques

Verification and validation (V&V) techniques are used to check whether a system conforms to the requirements and whether it satisfies its intended use. Verification and validation techniques are used in all kinds of domains. However, the interpretation of notions and central concepts varies in different communities. In this section, we first give a brief introduction to some basic ideas and review the main characteristics of important V&V techniques. Then, we introduce the techniques that are most relevant for the approach of this thesis, namely model checking and conformance testing.

2.3.1 Preliminaries

For software validation and verification, there exists an IEEE standard [IEE04], which gives the following definitions:

- Validation: *The process of evaluating a system or component during or at the end of the development process to determine whether it satisfies specified requirements.* (Are we building the right thing?)

- Verification: *The process of evaluating a system or component to determine whether the products of a given development phase satisfy the conditions imposed at the start of that phase.* (Are we building the thing rightly?)

Unfortunately, the IEEE classification of Validation and Verification is not always in compliance to the use of the terms in different communities. For example, an alternative interpretation that is wide-spread in software engineering communities is to take the term verification literally. Then, it corresponds to formal proof techniques that aim at yielding absolute guarantees about the correctness of a given system, in contrast to falsification techniques such as simulation and testing. In the HW/SW co-design community, the differentiation between verification and validation is often abandoned, and the term HW/SW co-verification is used for all kinds of V&V techniques. To simplify things and to stay out of the debate, we follow this and use the term *co-verification* for all kinds of V&V techniques applied to the HW/SW co-design domain.

In general, one can distinguish *static* and *dynamic* V&V techniques. Static V&V techniques are static analyses and formal verification, the most popular dynamic V&V techniques are simulation and testing. In this thesis, we use formal verification, simulation and testing. *Formal verification* provides a formal proof that a formal specification satisfies a given property expressed as logic formula, using formal methods or mathematics. The result is *complete* and guarantees that the property is satisfied for all possible input scenarios. Important formal verification techniques are *model checking* and *theorem proving*. In *simulation and testing*, experiments are performed before deploying the system in the field. In *simulation*, the experiments are performed on a model or abstraction of the system. *Testing* is similar to simulation, apart from that the experiments are performed with the real implementation. The border between simulation and testing becomes blurred in mixed HW/SW systems because very often parts of the system are simulated while for others the implementation is executed. Common examples are *Hardware in the Loop* simulations, where the real hardware is executed in a simulated environment, and *Software in the Loop* simulations, where the software is executed on simulated hardware. The main advantage of simulation and testing techniques is that they do not require any prerequisites like a formal system model or formal

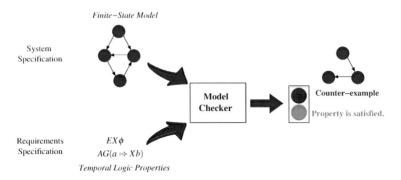

Figure 2.5: Model Checking

requirement specifications, and that the effort is considerably lower than for formal verification. The disadvantage is that the results are *incomplete*, yielding only propositions with respect to the executed input scenarios. In other words, simulation and testing can be used to show the presence of bugs, but never their absence (Dijkstra [DHD72]). Note that all V&V techniques can be used for both verification or validation. With formal verification, one can prove that a system fulfills a given requirements specification or that a refined formal model conforms to an abstract specification. Regarding simulation and testing, one can check certain *assertions* during test execution, which are derived from the requirements specification (*assertion-based testing*), or one can compare the outputs of an implementation with the outputs of a specification (*specification-based testing*). Checking whether the implementation conforms to the specification is a special case of specification-based testing also termed *conformance testing*.

2.3.2 Model Checking

The aim of model checking is to check whether a model of a finite-state concurrent system (system specification) fulfills certain logical properties (requirement specification). A *model checker* is a tool that automatically checks whether the properties are satisfied, and yields counter-examples if not (see Figure 2.5). The counter-examples are given as *traces* of the system that violate the postulated property. The following section gives a brief introduction to model checking based on Clarke et al. [CGP99].

Formally, model checking is used to check whether a model $\mathcal{M}$ satisfies a property ϕ:

$$\mathcal{M} \models \phi$$

The model $\mathcal{M}$ of the system is usually specified as a labeled transition system (LTS), which can be represented as a *Kripke structure*. A Kripke structure is a labeled transition graph, where the nodes represent the reachable states of the system and the edges transitions from one state to another. Paths in the graph model possible executions of the system. To model properties of the system, a function is used that labels each state with a set of atomic propositions that are true in this state. Formally, a Kripke structure $\mathcal{M}$ can be defined as follows:

Definition 1 (Kripke Structure). *Let AP be a set of atomic propositions. A Kripke structure $\mathcal{M}$ over AP is a four tuple $\mathcal{M} = (S, S_0, R, L)$ where*

- *S is a finite set of states,*

- *$S_0 \subseteq S$ is the set of initial states,*

- *$R \subseteq S \times S$ is a transition relation that must be total, i. e., for every state $s \in S$ there is state $s' \in S$ such that $R(s, s')$,*

- *$L : S \rightarrow 2^{AP}$ is a function that labels each state with the set of atomic propositions true in that state.*

A path in $\mathcal{M}$ is an infinite sequence of states $\pi = s_0 s_1 s_2 ...$ such that $R(s_i, s_{i+1})$ for all $i \geq 0$.

For the specification of logical properties of both hardware and software systems, temporal logics have proved to be useful. With temporal properties, it is possible to describe the ordering of events in time without introducing time explicitly. Temporal logics use atomic propositions and boolean operations to describe properties of states (such as *"situation is critical"*), and *temporal operators* such as *eventually* or *never* to describe properties beyond states (such as *"a critical situation **never** arises"*). A logic for specifying properties of the state transition systems is the computation tree logic CTL*, which is used to describe properties of *computation trees*. A computation tree can be derived from a labeled transition system by taking the initial state as root, and then appending all possible successor states of the system. To those, again the successor states are appended until all (infinite) paths of the system are unfolded. An example is shown in Figure 2.6. From the initial node a, possible successor states are b and c. From state b, one can only go back to a, from state c to b or c, and so on.

CTL* formulae are composed of a *state formula*, which describe properties of a state, *temporal operators*, which describe properties of a path, and *path quantifiers*, which describe whether a property holds on all path or on some path. There are two path quantifiers and five basic temporal operators in CTL*:

- Path quantifiers:

  - **A**: *for all paths* (**A**lways)

  - **E**: *for some path* (**E**xists)

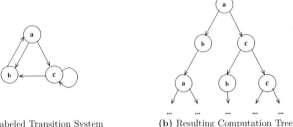

(a) Labeled Transition System   (b) Resulting Computation Tree

Figure 2.6: Computation Tree

- Temporal operators:

  - **X** ϕ: property ϕ holds in the next state (ne**X**t)

  - **F** ϕ: property ϕ will hold at some state in the future (**F**uture)

  - **G** ϕ: property ϕ holds at every state (**G**lobally)

  - ϕ_1 **U** ϕ_2: property ϕ_1 holds in all states until property ϕ_2 holds (**U**ntil), and ϕ_2 holds eventually at some state

  - ϕ_1 **R** ϕ_2: property ϕ_2 holds in all states until property ϕ_1 holds, or ϕ_2 holds never (**R**elease)

In CTL*, these operators can be freely combined. The most important subsets of CTL* are the *linear-time logic* LTL and the *computation tree logic* CTL. LTL is based on the assumption that time is linear and thus only a single path is considered. As a consequence, no path quantifiers are used in LTL.[4] In this thesis, we focus on CTL because the UPPAAL requirements language is a subset of CTL.[5] In CTL, it is assumed that there are branches in the computation tree, and temporal operators must be immediately preceded by a path quantifier. This leads to the following rules for the structure of CTL formulae:

- if $p \in AP$, then p is a state formula

- if ϕ_1, ϕ_2 are state formulae, then $\neg\phi_1, \phi_1 \wedge \phi_2$ and $\phi_1 \vee \phi_2$ are state formulae

- if ϕ_1, ϕ_2 are state formulae, then **X** ϕ_1, **F** ϕ_1, **G** ϕ_1, ϕ_1 **U** ϕ_2, and ϕ_1 **R** ϕ_2 are path formulae

- if ϕ is a path formula, then **E** ϕ and **A** ϕ are state formulae

---

[4]LTL can nevertheless be applied to computation trees. Then, an implicit **A**lways is assumed and the given property must hold on all paths.

[5]In UPPAAL, nesting of path formulae is not allowed. As a consequence, complex properties such as confluence cannot be verified.

Using CTL it is possible to specify important properties, in particular *safety properties* (something bad will never happen), and *liveness properties* (something good will eventually happen).

The simplest model checking algorithm is to construct an explicit representation of a Kripke structure $\mathcal{M} = (S, R, L)$ as a labeled, directed graph, and then to check which states in S satisfy a CTL formula ϕ. The problem is that the explicit representation of the Kripke structure yields an exponential increase in the number of states, which is also referred to as the *state space explosion* problem. Several techniques exist to face this problem, e.g., *binary decision diagrams, symbolic model checking, partial order reduction,* and *abstraction techniques*. However, to elaborate these techniques is not in the scope of this thesis. We refer the interested reader to Clarke et al. [CGP99].

2.3.3 Conformance Testing

The aim of conformance testing is to determine whether an implementation of a system conforms to its specification. To this end, it is a necessary prerequisite to define a formal *implementation relation*. Widely used and well-established in the context of model-based testing of labeled transition systems is the *input output conformance* (ioco) relation introduced by Tretmans [Tre96]. In this section, we briefly review the *ioco*-theory. For more detail, we refer to Schmaltz et al. [ST08] and Tretmans [Tre08].

An implementation relation relates an implementation to its specification. Whereas a specification is a formal object taken from a formal domain *SPEC*, the implementation is usually a real physical object. To relate such an implementation to a formal specification is possible by assuming that any real implementation can be modeled by some formal object $i \in MOD$, where *MOD* is the universe of all possible implementation models. This assumption is usually referred to as the *test assumption*. Based on the test assumption, a formal implementation relation can be defined as $imp \in MOD \times SPEC$. An implementation i is than said to be correct with respect to a specification s if $i \, imp \, s$.

The implementation relation *ioco* is based on the assumption that both the specification and the implementation can be described by labeled transition systems (LTS) with inputs and outputs. The *ioco* relation defines that an implementation i conforms to its specification s if any experiment derived from s and executed on i leads to an output of i that is foreseen by s.

Definition 2 (Input-output conformance (ioco)). *An implementation i conforms to a specification s if for all input traces σ that can be derived from s the set of output traces of i is contained in the set of all possible output traces of s:*

$$i \; ioco \; s \quad iff \;\; \forall \sigma \in traces(s) : out(i \; after \; \sigma) \subseteq out(s \; after \; \sigma)$$

The domains of i and s, and also the semantics of *traces*(s) and *out*(s, σ) are defined by the type and interpretation of the labeled transition system used for modeling implementation and specification. For now, we deliberately abstract away from any specific semantics. In Chapter 6, we describe a more specific conformance relation for UPPAAL timed automata.

Based on the *ioco* relation it is possible to evaluate test results by comparing the outputs of the implementation with those predicted by the specification. If the implementation sends an output not foreseen by the specification, the test verdict is *fail*. If the implementation sends only expected outputs for a given input trace, the test verdict is *pass*. A peculiar aspect of the *ioco* relation is that the absence of outputs is also considered as an observable event, which is called *quiescence*. This allows the definition of a timeout if the implementation does not send any outputs for a certain time interval, after which the test verdict is *fail*.

From the *ioco* relation, a general approach for the generation of conformance tests can be derived. First, one has to compute all possible output traces of the specification for a given input trace. Second, the implementation is executed for the same input trace. The previously computed output traces can then be used as a *test oracle* to check the correctness of the outputs of the specification using the relation $out(i\ after\ \sigma) \subseteq out(s\ after\ \sigma)$. This can be done fully automatically. Tretmans [Tre08] showed that the generated tests are *sound*, i.e., any failing implementation is indeed non-conforming and no false detections of errors can be made.

2.4 SystemC

SystemC [IEE05] was introduced by the Open SystemC Initiative (OSCI) in 1999[6]. The aim of the Open SystemC Initiative was to develop an open industry standard for system-level modeling, design and verification. SystemC can be seen as both a system level design language and a framework for HW/SW co-simulation. It allows the modeling and execution of system level designs on various levels of abstraction, including classical register transfer level hardware modeling and transaction-based design. This allows system-level design from abstract concept down to implementation in a unified framework. Note that SystemC without extensions can only be used for *digital* HW/SW Systems. There also exists an extension for analog and mixed-signal components, namely SystemC-AMS, but this is not in the scope of this thesis.

SystemC is implemented as a C++ class library, which provides the language elements and an event-driven simulation kernel. The language comprises constructs for modularization and structuring, for hardware, software and communication modeling, and for synchronization and coordination of concurrent processes. From a structural point of view, a SystemC design is a set of modules, connected by channels. The structure strictly separates between computation and communication units (i. e., modules and channels) and is highly

---

[6]Corporate OSCI members are amongst others: ARM, Intel, Cadence, CoWare, NXP, Synopsis, Mentor Graphics, and STMicroelectronics.

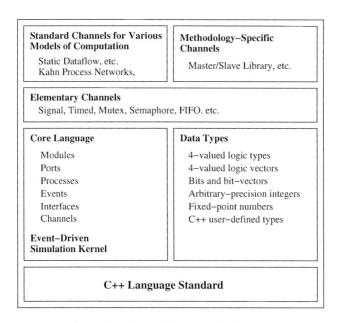

Figure 2.7: SystemC Language Architecture

flexible due to a communication concept that allows transaction level modeling and communication refinement. The event-driven simulation kernel regards the SystemC design as a set of concurrent processes that are synchronized and coordinated by events and communicate through channels.

The SystemC language architecture is shown in Figure 2.7. The SystemC language provides constructs for the modeling of concurrency, time, reactivity, hardware data types, hierarchy and communication. As SystemC is implemented as a C++ class library, the C++ language standard constitutes the base of the language architecture. Above that, the core language of SystemC provides means to describe the *structure* and the *behavior* of a system. The structure is described by using modules, channels, ports, and interfaces, the *behavior* by using processes and events. Together with the event-driven simulation kernel, the core language defines the semantics of SystemC. Alongside to that, the SystemC language provides a set of hardware data-types. On top of the core language and the dedicated hardware data-types, a set of elementary channels is defined, which can be used for more specific models of computation, e. g., FIFOs for functional or signals for hardware modeling. The topmost layer of the SystemC language architecture consists of design libraries and models needed for more specific design methodologies or models of computation. Note that those are not part of the SystemC standard. The SystemC standard [IEE05] comprises the core language together with the event-driven simulation kernel, the dedicated data-types, and the elementary channels. The

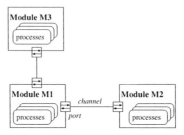

Figure 2.8: Structure of a SystemC Design

aim of this section is to give a sufficient overview of SystemC to understand
the remainder of this thesis. For a more elaborated introduction to SystemC,
please refer to Groetker [Gro02] and Black et al. [BD05]. In the following, we
describe both the structure and the behavior of a SystemC design and briefly
review the simulation semantics.

2.4.1 Structural Modeling

From a structural point of view, a SystemC design consists of a set of *modules*,
connected by *channels*. An example is shown in Figure 2.8. The separation of
modules and channels allows the separation of *computation* and *communica-*
tion. Together with a flexible communication model based on channels, ports,
and interfaces, this allows *transaction level modeling* with SystemC. It also
enables the use of many different models of computation. In the following,
we first describe the basic structure of modules, and then the communication
model based on channels, ports, and interfaces. Then, we introduce two special kinds of channels, namely hierarchical and primitive channels. Finally, we
describe how a design is composed by instantiating modules and channels and
by binding the module ports to the channels.

Modules   Modules are the basic building blocks that allow a modular and
hierarchical design. Each module contains a set of *ports*, through which the
module communicates with other modules, a set of *processes*, which describe
the functionality and behavior of the module, and a set of *data variables* and
internal channels that can be used to store the module's state and for internal
communication between the module's processes. In addition, a module may
contain other modules.

Communication Model   To interconnect modules, SystemC uses interfaces,
ports, and channels. The communication concept is shown in Figure 2.9. Ports
are used as communication interface of a module, i. e., they define entry points
for communication. Each port is bound to an interface, which defines a set

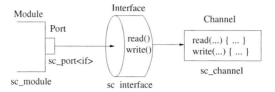

Figure 2.9: SystemC Communication Concept

of virtual communication methods. This declares the communication methods that can be accessed via the port. Whereas ports and interfaces define which communication methods a module may use, channels are used to implement the communication methods. A channel implements an interface, if it provides an implementation for each virtual method declared in the interface. The main advantage of the SystemC communication concept based is that the structure is highly modular and supports communication refinement. Following the idea of transaction level modeling, communication and computation are strictly separated in SystemC designs. As a consequence, it is possible to exchange a channel without touching the modules connected by the channel if the ports and interfaces are unchanged. For example, the abstract *read* and *write* methods declared in Figure 2.9 could be first implemented as a simple copy operation on abstract data variables in an abstract design, and later be replaced by a bit-accurate register transfer or a complex bus system. Note that the abstract channel concept allows the implementation of many models of computation in SystemC. If transactors are used that translate between different models of computations or different abstraction levels, the SystemC communication concept can also be used for multi-level simulations.

Hierarchical and Primitive Channels   There are two special types of channels: *hierarchical channels* and *primitive channels*. A hierarchical channel is one which contains embedded modules or channels. Hierarchical channels allow the modeling of complex communication structures such as the *on-chip bus* (OCB) or *communication area network* (CAN) buses. A primitive channel is defined as a channel which supports the *request-update* scheme. The *request-update* scheme is closely related to the *delta-cycles* used by the SystemC simulation kernel to simulate concurrency. The idea is that for the simulation of concurrent activities on a single CPU, it is necessary to serialize the activities. To impose a partial order on concurrent activities, the execution is split into delta-cycles, which consist if an evaluate phase and an update phase. Together with the request-update scheme supported by primitive channels, this allows deterministic serialization of concurrent activities: In the evaluate phase, processes are executed, but the results do not change the internal state of primitive channels. Instead, a *request_update* function is called to postpone the update of the channel state. The actual update is not performed until the update phase, which is started only when all processes are evaluated. This ensures that the order in which processes are executed

Figure 2.10: Producer-Consumer Example

does not matter, assuming that no implicit communication (through shared variables) is used and that all communications between concurrent processes actually are implemented by primitive channels.

As an example for the structure of a SystemC design, see Figure 2.10. A producer and a consumer module are connected through a FIFO channel. The producer uses a *write* method to put tokens into the FIFO buffer, the consumer gets them using a *read* method. The SystemC code for the declaration of the producer and consumer modules is shown in Listing 2.1 and Listing 2.2. Both modules are equipped with two ports, one which is connected to a clock, and one that is bound to the FIFO interface. A process *SC_THREAD* is used to implement the functionality.

A possible definition of the FIFO interface and the FIFO channel is given in Listing 2.3. The interface *fifo_if* is derived from the abstract base class *sc_interface* and defines the virtual *read* and *write* methods, in this case using integers as data type. The channel implementation is derived from the abstract base class *sc_channel* and the FIFO interface. Besides the constructor, it contains internal variables and events, and the implementation of the *read* and *write* methods.

Instantiation and Binding For simulation, modules and channels have to be instantiated and ports must be bound to channels. This is usually done either in a top-level design, or in the *sc_main* method, which also starts the simulation. Listing 2.4 shows an exemplary main method for the producer-consumer example. A clock *clk* is instantiated using the SystemC type *sc_clock*,

```
SC_MODULE( producer )
{
  sc_port<sc_clock> p_clock;
  sc_port<fifo_if> fifo;

  SC_CTOR( producer )
  {
    SC_THREAD( main_method );
    sensitive << p_clock;
  }
};
```

Listing 2.1: Producer Module

```
SC_MODULE( consumer )
{
  sc_port<sc_clock> c_clock;
  sc_port<fifo_if> fifo;

  SC_CTOR( consumer )
  {
    SC_THREAD( main_method );
    sensitive << c_clock;
  }
};
```

Listing 2.2: Consumer Module

```
class fifo_if :
  virtual public sc_interface
{
  public:
    virtual void write(int c) = 0;
    virtual int read(void) = 0;
};

class fifo :
  public sc_channel, public fifo_if
{
  // internal variables and events
  private:
    int buffer[SIZE];
    int n, r_pos, w_pos;
  public:
    sc_event w_event, r_event;

    // constructor
    fifo(sc_module_name name) :
      sc_channel(name), n(0), r_pos(0), w_pos(0) {}

  // implementation of read and write method

};
```

Listing 2.3: FIFO Interface and Channel

```
int sc_main(int argc, char* argv[])
{
  // clock generation
  sc_clock clk("clk", 50, SC_NS);

  // module and channel instantiation
  producer prod_inst("producer");
  consumer cons_inst("consumer");
  fifo fifo_inst("fifo");

  // port binding
  prod_inst.p_clock(clk);
  prod_inst.fifo(fifo_inst);
  cons_inst.c_clock(clk);
  cons_inst.fifo(fifo_inst);

  // run simulation for 1000 ms
  sc_start(1000, SC_MS);
  return 0;
}
```

Listing 2.4: Main Method

which is parameterized with the desired clock frequency (50 ns). The producer and consumer modules and the FIFO channel are instantiated, and the ports are bound to the clock and the FIFO channel. Finally, the simulation is run for 1000 ms using the *sc_start* method. Note that generally all ports must be bound, or a design cannot be executed. This implies that SystemC designs that interact with their environment can only be executed together with a test bench that provides the inputs and observes the outputs.

2.4.2 Behavioral Modeling

SystemC designs are executed in a discrete-event simulation. The basic execution unit are processes, which are triggered by events. Thus, from a behavioral point of view, a SystemC design can be regarded as a network of concurrent processes, which communicate through channels and synchronize on events. In the following, we describe the main concepts of processes and events and how they are used in the discrete-event simulation.

Processes Processes are contained in modules and use the ports of the containing module to access external channels. SystemC provides two kinds of processes: *method processes* and *thread processes*. A *method process*, when triggered, always executes its body from the beginning to the end and does not keep an internal execution state. It is not possible to suspend and resume a method process. In contrast to that, a *thread process* can be suspended at any time by calling a *wait* function. It keeps its internal execution state and thus can be resumed at the point where it was suspended. Note that a thread process is only started once at the beginning of simulation, whereas a method process may be invoked arbitrary often.

The functionality of processes is described in *methods*, which contain the executable code of a SystemC design. For execution, the methods are encapsulated into processes, which care for the interactions with the scheduler and the events. As a consequence, methods are either invoked by the encapsulating process, or called by other methods. This includes communication methods, which are called as external methods through the port their channel is bound to. In Listing 2.1 and Listing 2.2, the method *main_method* is encapsulated into a thread process using the *SC_THREAD* macro. A similar macro exists for method processes (*SC_METHOD*).

Events Both thread and method processes are triggered by *events*. An *event* is an object that determines whether and when a process would be triggered. The triggering of an event is called *event notification*. Whenever an event is notified, this triggers the execution of all processes that are *sensitive* to the event. A process may be sensitive to an event either statically or dynamically. Static sensitivity is allowed for both method and thread processes, dynamic sensitivity is only allowed for thread processes. A static sensitivity list is attached to a process statically within the module constructor, as an example

wait(e)	wait for event e to be notified
wait(t)	wait for t time units to elapse
wait(t,e)	wait for event e for maximally t time units
wait()	wait for any event from the static sensitivity list
wait(e1 & e2 & e3)	wait for all three events to be notified
wait(e1 | e2 | e3)	wait for any of the three events to be notified

Table 2.1: Variants of the *wait* Statement

see Listing 2.1 and Listing 2.2, where their static sensitivity lists consist in each case only of the clock event. A static sensitivity list may also contain multiple events. A method process is triggered, whenever an event from its static sensitivity list is notified. While method processes are executed from the beginning to the end whenever an event from their static sensitivity list occurs, thread processes may suspend execution by calling a *wait* function. This overwrites their static sensitivity list temporarily and is called dynamic sensitivity. For example, if a process calls *wait(e)*, it becomes sensitive to the event e and is resumed at the next occurrence (i. e., notification) of the event e. A process can also be dynamically sensitive to multiple events or for the elapsing of a certain amount of time. Table 2.1 shows the variants of *wait* calls available in SystemC. As a thread process either runs or is suspended, the only possibility to wait for an event from the static sensitivity list in a thread process is to suspend it with an empty *wait()* statement. If an event object e is notified by its owner, processes that are sensitive to the event start resp. resume execution. SystemC supports three types of event notifications. An *immediate notification*, invoked by `e.notify()`, causes processes to be triggered immediately in the current delta cycle. A *delta-delay notification*, invoked by `e.notify(0)`, causes processes to be triggered at the same time instant, but after updating primitive channels, i. e., in the next delta-cycle. A *timed notification*, invoked by `e.notify(t)` with `t > 0`, causes processes to be triggered after the given delay `t`. If an event is notified that already has a pending notification, only the notification with the earliest expiration time takes effect. That means that immediate notifications override all pending notifications, delta-delay notifications override timed notifications, and timed notifications override pending timed notifications if their delay expires earlier.

The behavior of the producer-consumer example is defined in four methods: the *main_method*s of the producer and the consumer module, and the read and write methods of the FIFO channel. Listing 2.5 and Listing 2.6 show the *main_method*s. As thread processes are only started once at the beginning of simulation, an unconditionally executed while-loop is needed for infinite execution. Within the while loop, the processes wait to be triggered by events from their static sensitivity list, i. e., *p_clock* and *c_clock*. Every time they are triggered, the producer produces a token and writes it to the FIFO, while the consumer reads a token from the FIFO and consumes it. Note that the *read*

```
void main_method(void)              void main_method(void)
{                                   {
  int c = 0;                          int c = 0;
  while(true)                         while(true)
  {                                   {
    wait();                             wait();
    // produce c                        c = fifo ->read();
    fifo ->write(c);                    // consume c
  }                                   }
}                                   }
```

Listing 2.5: Producer Method   Listing 2.6: Consumer Method

and *write* methods of the FIFO are blocking, as can be seen in Listing 2.7 and Listing 2.8. The *read* and *write* methods are synchronized using the events *r_event* and *w_event*. Whenever the FIFO buffer is full ($n == SIZE$), the *write* method calls *wait(r_event)*. By this, the calling process (i. e., the producer) is blocked until the event *r_event* is notified. This is done by the *read* (i. e., the consumer) method by calling *r_event.notify()*, whenever a token is read from the buffer . On the other hand, the *read* method is blocked whenever the buffer is empty ($n == 0$) and released by the event *w_event* which is notified by the producer whenever a token is written.

2.4.3 Simulation Semantics

The execution of a SystemC design is controlled by the SystemC scheduler. It controls the simulation time, the execution of processes, handles event notifications and updates primitive channels. Like typical hardware description languages, SystemC supports the notion of delta-cycles. Delta-cycles are used to impose a partial order on simultaneous actions and split the concurrent execution of processes into two phases. In the first phase, concurrent processes

```
void write(int c)                   int read(void)
{                                   {
                                      int c;
  if (n == SIZE)                      if (n == 0)
    wait(r_event);                      wait(w_event);
  buffer[w_pos] = c;                  c = buffer[r_pos];
  n = n + 1;                          n = n - 1;
  w_pos = (w_pos + 1)%SIZE;           r_pos = (r_pos + 1)%SIZE;
  w_event.notify();                   r_event.notify();
                                      return c;
}                                   }
```

Listing 2.7: Write Method   Listing 2.8: Read Method

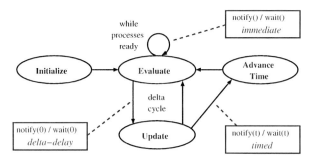

Figure 2.11: SystemC Scheduler

are evaluated, i.e., their method body is executed. This may include read
and write accesses to primitive channels, which store changes in temporary
variables. In the second phase, the actual channel state is updated. A delta-
cycle lasts an infinitesimal amount of time, and an arbitrary, finite number of
delta-cycles may be executed at one point in simulation time. Note that the
order in which processes are executed within a delta-cycle is not specified in
[IEE05], i.e., it is inherently *non-deterministic*. The same holds for the order
of the updates of primitive channels.

The simulation semantics can be summarized as follows:

(i) *Initialization*: each process is executed once,

(ii) *Evaluation*: all processes ready to run are executed in arbitrary order,
if there are immediate notifications, the corresponding processes become
ready to run as well and are immediately executed,

(iii) *Update*: primitive channels are updated,

(iv) if there are delta-delay notifications, the corresponding processes are triggered and steps 2 and 3 are repeated,

(v) if there are timed notifications, simulation time is advanced to the earliest
pending timed notification and steps 2 – 4 are repeated,

(vi) if there are no remaining notifications, simulation is finished.

Figure 2.11 illustrates the behavior of the SystemC scheduler. For a more
comprehensive description of the SystemC simulation semantics, we refer to
Groetker [Gro02], Müller et al. [MRR03], and Ruf et al. [RHG⁺01].

2.5 Uppaal Timed Automata

Timed Automata were introduced by Alur et al. [AD94] as a timed extension of the classical finite state automata. A notion of time is introduced by

clock variables, which are used in clock constraints to model time-dependent behavior. Systems comprising multiple concurrent processes are modeled by networks of timed automata, which are executed with interleaving semantics and synchronize on channels. UPPAAL [BLL⁺95, BY04, BDL04] is a tool set for the modeling, simulation, animation and verification of networks of timed automata. The UPPAAL model checker enables the verification of temporal properties, including safety and liveness properties. The simulator can be used to visualize counter-examples produced by the model checker. In the following, we first introduce the semantics of Timed Automata and Networks of Timed Automata. Then, we review the main concepts used for a symbolic semantics of timed automata, and introduce difference bound matrices. Finally, we describe some specialties and extensions of the UPPAAL modeling language.

2.5.1 Timed Automata

As typical state automata, timed automata consist of a set of nodes, which are called *locations* and which are connected by *edges*. A notion of time is introduced by a set of real-valued clock variables $C : \mathbb{R}_{\geq 0}$. They are used in clock constraints to model time-dependent behavior. The clocks are initialized with zero and then run synchronously with the same speed. As an effect of a transition, a clock may be reseted, i.e., set to zero. A clock constraint is a conjunctive formula of atomic constraints of the form $x \sim n$ or $x - y \sim n$ for $x, y \in C, \sim \in \{\leq, <, =, >, \geq\}, n \in \mathbb{N}$. $B(C)$ denotes the set of clock constraints. In *Timed Büchi Automata*, clock constraints are assigned to edges and are interpreted as enabling conditions for the corresponding transitions. They cannot force the transition to be taken. As a consequence, a Timed Büchi Automaton may stay an infinite amount of time in the same location. Alur et al. [AD94] solved this problem by *Büchi acceptance conditions*. A subset of locations is marked as accepting, and only executions passing through an accepting location infinitely often are considered as valid behaviors. A more intuitive solution to the problem of infinite idling is given by Henzinger et al. [HNSY94] by introducing *Timed Safety Automata*. In Timed Safety Automata, one can distinguish two kinds of clock constraints: *Guards* are assigned to edges and yield conditions, under which the corresponding transition may be taken. In other words, they *enable* progress. *Invariants* are assigned to locations and yield conditions, under which one may stay in the corresponding state. The *invariants* must not be violated, i.e., the location must be left before its invariant is invalidated. In other words, invariants *ensure* progress. In the remainder of this thesis, we refer to *Timed Safety Automata* whenever we use the term *timed automata*.

A simple example for a timed automaton is shown in Figure 2.12. It consists of two locations l_0 and l_1 that are connected by two edges from l_0 to l_1. To l_0 and l_1, the same invariant $x \leq 1$ is assigned. That means that in both locations, the automaton may stay at most for one time unit. The upper edge from l_0 to l_1 has a guard $x == 1$, and the clock y is reseted, whenever this edge is taken. The lower edge from l_0 to l_1 has a guard $x \leq 1$ and no effect. As a consequence, there are two possibilities to come from location l_0 to location l_1: during time

Figure 2.12: Example: A Simple Timed Automaton

$x \in [0,1]$, the lower edge may fire without effect, and at $x = 1$, the upper edge may fire and y is reset.

More formally, a timed automaton can be defined following Bengtsson et al. [BLL+95] and Behrmann et al. [BDL04]:

Definition 3 (Formal Syntax of a Timed Automaton). *A timed automaton is a tuple* (L, l_0, C, A, E, I), *where*

- L *is a set of locations,* $l_0 \in L$ *the initial location,*

- C *is a set of clocks,* A *a set of actions,*

- $I : L \rightarrow B(C)$ *assigns invariants to locations, and*

- $E \subseteq L \times B(C) \times A \times \mathbb{P}^C \times L$ *is a set of edges. We use the notion* $l \xrightarrow{g,a,r} l'$ *for* $(l, g, a, r, l') \in E$.

The semantics of a timed automaton is defined as a transition system where a state (l, u) consists of a location l and a clock valuation u. The clock valuation u maps all clocks in C to non-negative real values. We use the term $u \in g$ to denote that all clock values satisfy the guard g, and the term $u + d$ with $d \in \mathbb{R}_{\geq 0}$ to denote a mapping of all clocks $x \in C$ to $u(x) + d$. Furthermore, we denote resetting of clocks with $u' = [r \mapsto 0]u$, where all clocks in $r \subseteq C$ are set to zero. Based on that, we can define the operational semantics of a timed automaton:

Definition 4 (Operational Semantics of a Timed Automaton). *The semantics of a timed automaton* (L, l_0, C, A, E, I) *is defined as a transition system* $(S, s_0, \rightarrow)$, *where* $S \subseteq L \times \mathbb{R}_{\geq 0}^{|C|}$ *is a set of states,* $s_0 = (l_0, u_0)$ *the initial state, and* $\rightarrow \subseteq S \times (\mathbb{R}_{\geq 0} \cup A) \times S$ *the transition relation. A semantic step of a timed timed automaton can either be a time step (1) or a discrete transition (2) along an edge in the graphical representation:*

(1) $(l, u) \xrightarrow{d} (l, u + d)$ *iff* $\forall d' : 0 \leq d' \leq d \Rightarrow u + d' \in I(l)$

(2) $(l, u) \xrightarrow{a} (l', u')$ *iff* $\exists l \xrightarrow{g,a,r} l'$ *such that* $u \in g \wedge u' = [r \mapsto 0]u \wedge u' \in I(l')$

Based on the operational semantics, we can define a *run* of a timed automaton as a sequence of transitions. A run of a timed automaton is defined over a *timed trace*. A timed trace is a (possibly infinite) sequence of *timed actions*. A timed action is a pair (t, a), where the action $a \in A$ is taken by a timed automaton after $t \in \mathbb{R}_{\geq 0}$ time units after the automaton was started. The absolute time t is also called *time stamp* of a.

Definition 5 (Timed Traces). *A timed trace is a (possibly infinite) sequence of timed actions:*

$$ttr = (t_1, a_1)(t_2, a_2)...(t_i, a_i)...$$

where $t_i \leq t_{i+1}$ for all $i \geq 1$.

Using the notion of a timed trace, we can define a *run of a timed automaton.*

Definition 6 (Run of a Timed Automaton). *A run of a timed automaton over a timed trace $ttr = (t_1, a_1)(t_2, a_2)(t_3, a_3)...$ is a sequence of transitions:*

$$(l_0, u_0) \xrightarrow{d_1, a_1} (l_1, u_1) \xrightarrow{d_2, a_2} (l_2, u_2) \xrightarrow{d_3, a_3} (l_3, u_3)...$$

where $t_i = t_{i-1} + d_i$, $t_0 = 0$ for all $i \geq 1$.

Based on the definition of the syntax and semantics of a single timed automaton, we can define the semantics of networks of timed automata.

2.5.2 Networks of Timed Automata

Networks of timed automata are used to model systems with concurrent processes. The state of a network of timed automata is defined as a vector of the current locations of all timed automata in the network and all clock valuations. For synchronization, the automata may interchange events. An event is sent over a channel c, and $c!$ and $c?$ denote sending resp. receiving an event. Formally, the semantics of a network of timed automata is given by Bengtsson et al. [BY04] as follows:

Definition 7 (Semantics of a Network of Timed Automata). *A network of timed automata (NTA) consists of n timed automata $\mathscr{A}_i = (L_i, l_i^0, C, A, E_i, I_i)$. The semantics of NTA is defined by a transition system $(S, s_0, \rightarrow)$. Each state $s \in S$ is a tuple $(\bar{l}, u)$, where $\bar{l}$ is a location vector and u a clock valuation. $S = (L_1 \times ... \times L_n) \times \mathbb{R}_{\geq 0}^{|C|}$ denotes the set of states, $s_0 = (\bar{l}_0, u_0)$ the initial state, and $\rightarrow \subseteq S \times S$ the transition relation. Furthermore, τ denotes an internal action, $c!, c?$ sending resp. receiving an event, g a clock guard, and $u' = [r \mapsto 0]u$ denotes a clock valuation where all clocks from r are reset to zero. A semantic step can be either a time step (1), an independent step of a single automaton (2), or a synchronization between two automata (3):*

(1) $(\bar{l}, u) \rightarrow (\bar{l}, u + d)$ *iff* $\forall d' : 0 \leq d' \leq d \Rightarrow u + d' \in I(\bar{l})$

(2) $(\bar{l}, u) \rightarrow (\bar{l}[l_i'/l_i], u')$ *iff* $\exists l_i \xrightarrow{\tau g r} l_i'$ *such that* $u \in g \wedge u' = [r \mapsto 0]u \wedge u' \in I(\bar{l}[l_i'/l_i])$

(3) $(\bar{l}, u) \rightarrow (\bar{l}[l_j'/l_j, l_i'/l_i], u')$ *iff* $\exists l_i \xrightarrow{c?g_i, r_i} l_i' \wedge l_j \xrightarrow{c!g_j, r_j} l_j'$
such that $u \in (g_i \wedge g_j) \wedge u' = [r_i \cup r_j \mapsto 0]u \wedge u' \in I(\bar{l}')$

2.5.3 Symbolic Semantics of Timed Automata

The semantic state space of timed automata is infinite due to the real-valued clock variables. This makes it impossible to apply automatic verification techniques such as model checking, which explore the whole semantic state space. To solve this problem, the *symbolic semantics* presented by Bengtsson et al. [BLL+95] abstracts from certain points of time and uses clock zones instead. As a consequence, a state is then a tuple $(\bar{l}, D)$ where D is a difference bound matrix representing a clock zone. The resulting abstract model has a finite state space and can be model checked.

The foundation for a symbolic semantics of timed automata was laid by Alur et al. [AHH93]. There, the notion of *region equivalence* was introduced. The idea is that two clock assignments can be considered equivalent, if they have no influence on the possible transitions the timed automaton can take. If only integer variables are used in clock constraints that means that two clock assignments can be considered equivalent, when for each clock

- both are greater than a given maximal constant, also called *clock ceiling*
- their integer part is equal and both have a fractional part of zero, or
- their integer part is equal and both have a fractional part greater than zero.

In any case, the two clock assignments have to be in the same relation to all other clocks. This can be formalized as follows:

Definition 8 (Region equivalence). *Let k be a function, called a* clock ceiling, *that maps each clock $x \in C$ to a natural number $k(x)$. Furthermore, let $\{d\}$ denote the fractional part of a real number d, and $\lfloor d \rfloor$ denote its integer part. Two clock assignments u, v are region-equivalent $u \sim v$, iff*

(i) *their integer part is equal or both are greater than a given maximal constant, also called* clock ceiling:

$$\text{for all } x, \ \lfloor u(x) \rfloor = \lfloor v(x) \rfloor \quad \text{or} \quad u(x) > k(x) \wedge v(x) > k(x)$$

(ii) *both have a fractional part of zero or both have a fractional part greater than zero:*

$$\text{for all } x, \ \text{if } u(x) \leq k(x) \text{ then } \{u(x)\} = 0 \text{ iff } \{v(x)\} = 0$$

and

(iii) *both are in the same relation to all other clocks:*

$$\text{for all } x, y,$$
$$\text{if } u(x) \leq k(x) \wedge u(y) \leq k(y) \text{ then} \{u(x)\} \leq \{u(y)\} \text{ iff } \{v(x)\} \leq \{v(y)\}$$

Alur et al. [AD94] showed that for a fixed number of clocks and a given maximal constant, the number of regions is finite. Furthermore, $u \sim v$ implies that two states (l, u) and l, v are bisimilar w.r.t. the untimed bisimulation for any location or location vector of a timed automaton or a network of timed automata. As a consequence, region equivalence can be used for a finite-state partitioning of the infinite state space of timed automata. The finite-state model is called *region automaton* or *region graph*. Although the number of states in a region graph is finite, it is still exponential in the number of clocks.

A more efficient abstraction for timed automata is based on the notion of *zones* and *zone graphs*. A zone is a convex conjunction of a set of regions. If it is irrelevant for two possible semantic steps of a timed automation in which of a few regions a clock lies, these can be abstracted into one zone. In other words, a zone is the solution set of a clock constraint, i.e., the maximal set of clock assignments satisfying the constraint.

As an example, see the light switch controller in Figure 2.13 (taken from Bengtsson et al. [BLL+95]). The light switch controller waits for a press event. If the light switch is pressed twice within 10 time units, the light is dimmed. If the light switch is pressed only once, the light is switched on (location *bright*). Initially, the timed automaton in Figure 2.13a is in location *off*, and the clock x is zero. From that, there are two possible successor states: the automaton can perform a time step while staying in the same location or take the edge labeled with *press?* to the *dim* location. In the former case, there are infinitely many possibilities for the length of the delay. But, as the only possible discrete transition is along the edge labeled with *press?*, and as there is no clock constraint on that condition, it is irrelevant for the next semantic step how long the delay actually is. Thus, all possible successor states reached by a clock delay can be abstracted into one symbolic state with $x \geq 0$. From such abstractions, the zone graph can be constructed, as shown in Figure 2.13b. Each state in the zone graph consists of a location and a clock constraint representing a clock zone. Note that the region graph for the same example would range over more more than twenty clock regions and would be too large to be depicted here.

Based on the notion of clock zones and the corresponding definition of symbolic states as a pair (l, D) consisting of a location l and a clock zone D, the symbolic semantics of a timed automaton can be defined.

Definition 9 (Symbolic Semantics of a Timed Automaton). *The symbolic semantics of a timed automaton (L, l_0, C, A, E, I) is defined as a transition system $(S, s_0, \rightarrow)$, where $S \subseteq L \times B(C)$ is a set of symbolic states, $s_0 = (l_0, D_0)$ the initial symbolic state, and $\rightsquigarrow \subseteq S \times (B(C) \cup A) \times S$ is the symbolic transition relation over symbolic states. We denote an arbitrary delay with $D^{\uparrow} = \{u + d | u \in D, d \in \mathbb{R}_{\geq 0}\}$ and the reset function on a clock zone $r(D) = \{[r \mapsto 0]u | u \in D\}$. We denote the restriction of a clock zone with a set of constraints R with $D \wedge R$. A semantic step of a timed timed automaton can still either be a time step (1), now with an arbitrary delay that is allowed by the invariant of the current location, or a discrete transition (2) along an edge in the graphical representation.*

(1) $(l, D) \rightsquigarrow (l, D^{\uparrow} \wedge I(l))$

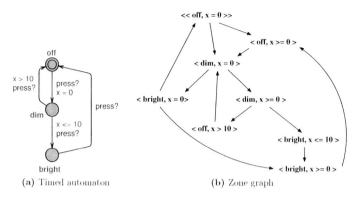

(a) Timed automaton   (b) Zone graph

Figure 2.13: Zone Graph Example

(2) $(l,D) \rightsquigarrow (l', r(D \wedge g) \wedge I(l'))$ if $l \overset{g,a,r}{\rightarrow} l'$

Note that the symbolic semantics is sound and complete, as shown by Bengtsson et al. [BLL$^+$95]. That means that for $u \in D$, $u' \in D'$, $(l,D) \rightsquigarrow (l',D')$ implies $(l,u) \rightarrow (l',u')$ for all $u' \in D'$ (soundness) and that $(l,u) \rightarrow (l',u')$ implies $(l,D) \rightsquigarrow (l',D')$ for some $u \in D$ (completeness).

Based on the definition of the symbolic semantics of a timed automaton, we can define *symbolic timed traces* as follows:

Definition 10 (Symbolic Timed Traces). *A symbolic timed trace is a (possibly infinite) sequence of timed actions, where the time is specified as a clock zone D:*

$$TTr = (D_1, a_1)(D_2, a_2)...(D_i, a_i)...$$

Using the notion of a symbolic timed trace, we can define a *symbolic execution of a timed automaton.*

Definition 11 (Run of a Timed Automaton). *A symbolic execution of a timed automaton over a symbolic timed trace $TTr = (D_1, a_1)(D_2, a_2)(D_3, a_3)...$ is a sequence of transitions:*

$$(l_0, D_0) \overset{d_1, a_1}{\rightarrow} (l_1, D_1) \overset{d_2, a_2}{\rightarrow} (l_2, D_2) \overset{d_3, a_3}{\rightarrow} (l_3, D_3)...$$

where $D_i = D_{i-1} + d_i$, $D_0 = 0$ for all $i \geq 1$.

2.5.4 Difference Bound Matrices

The symbolic semantics of timed automata is based on the notion of clock zones. An efficient representation of clock zones are *difference bound matrices*

(DBMs), presented by Bellman [Bel03]. Recall that a clock zone is the maximal set of clock assignments satisfying a given clock constraint. If a reference clock $\mathbf{0}$ with the constant value 0 is introduced, each clock constraint can be rewritten as a conjunction of atomic constraints of the form $x - y \sim n$. Note that two constraints referring to the same two clocks variables can be merged because only their intersection is relevant. As a consequence, each clock constraint can be rewritten as a conjunction of at most $(n + 1)^2$ atomic constraints. Thus, it is possible to store a clock zone in a $(n + 1) \times (n + 1)$ matrix, where each element represents an atomic constraint. Since each element in such a matrix corresponds to a bound on the difference between two clocks, they are named *Difference Bound Matrices* (DBM).

To construct a DBM, all clocks in C are indexed from 1 to n, and the index for $\mathbf{0}$ is 0. Then, in the DBM, the row i is used for the lower bounds on the difference between the clock with index i and all other clocks. Correspondingly, each column i is used for upper bounds on the difference between the clock with index i and all other clocks. In other words, for each constraint $x_i - x_j \sim n$, the element D_{ij} is set to $(n, \sim)$. To complete the DBM, for unbounded clock differences D_{ij} is set to ∞. Furthermore, the implicit constraints that all clocks are positive and that the difference between a clock and itself is zero are added by setting $D_{0i} = (0, \leq)$ and $D_{ii} = (0, \leq)$. As an example, consider the clock constraint $D = x < 20 \land y \leq 20 \land y - x \leq 10 \land y - x \geq 5 \land z > 5$. This can be rewritten as $D = x - \mathbf{0} < 20 \land y - \mathbf{0} \leq 20 \land y - x \leq 10 \land x - y \leq 5 \land \mathbf{0} - z < -5$. The resulting matrix representation is:

$$\begin{pmatrix} (0, \leq) & (0, \leq) & (-5, <) \\ (20, <) & (0, \leq) & (5, \leq) \\ (20, \leq) & (10, \leq) & (0, \leq) \end{pmatrix}$$

Note that one clock zone can be represented by an infinite number of DBMs. However, to yield a unique representation of clock zones, it is possible to use the tightest constraint on each clock difference. To compute the tightest constraints, a shortest path algorithm can be used, e. g., the Floyd-Warshall algorithm presented by Floyd [Flo62]. The resulting unique DBM is called a *canonical DBM*.

2.5.5 Uppaal

UPPAAL [BLL$^+$95, BY04, BDL04] is a tool set for the modeling, simulation, animation and verification of networks of timed automata. The UPPAAL model checker enables the verification of temporal properties, including safety and liveness properties. The simulator can be used to visualize counter-examples produced by the model checker.

Modeling Language

The UPPAAL modeling language extends timed automata by introducing parameterized timed automata templates, bounded integer variables, binary and broadcast channels, and urgent and committed location. Timed automata templates provide the possibility to model similar timed automata only once and to instantiate them arbitrary often with different parameters. Timed automata are modeled as a set of locations, connected by edges. The initial location is denoted by ⊚. Invariants can be assigned to locations and enforce that the location is left before they would be violated. Edges may be labeled with selections, guards, updates, and synchronizations. Selections are used to non-deterministically bind a given identifier to a value in a given range. Updates are used to reset clocks and to manipulate the data space, i.e., they provide the actions the automaton may perform. Processes synchronize by sending and receiving events through channels. Sending and receiving via a channel c is denoted by c! and c?, resp. Binary channels are used to synchronize one sender with a single receiver. A synchronization pair is chosen non-deterministically if more than one is enabled. If no communication partner is available, both the sender and the receiver are blocked if they synchronize on a binary channel. Broadcast channels are used to synchronize one sender with an arbitrary number of receivers. Any receiver that can synchronize must do so. In contrast to binary communication, a process sending on a broadcast channel is never blocked. Urgent and committed locations are used to model locations where no time may pass. Urgent locations are graphically depicted by the symbol ⊙, committed locations by the symbol ©. Leaving a committed location has priority over leaving non-committed locations.

A UPPAAL model comprises three parts: global declarations, parameterized timed automata (TA templates) and a system declaration. In the global declarations section, global variables, constants, channels and clocks are declared. The timed automata templates describe timed automata that can be instantiated with different parameters to model similar process. In the system declaration, the templates are instantiated and the system to be composed is given as a list of timed automata.

Query Language

The query language, which is used in UPPAAL to express requirements specifications, is a restricted version of CTL [BDL04]. Like in CTL, the query language consists of path formulae and state formulae. State formulae describe individual states, whereas path formulae quantify over paths of the model. Path formulae can be classified into reachability, safety and liveness.

State formulae are expressions that can be evaluated for a given state without looking at the rest of the model. This includes boolean expressions on variables (e.g., $x \leq 4$) and tests whether a particular process is in a given location (e.g., P1.init). A deadlock is expressed using the special state formula deadlock.

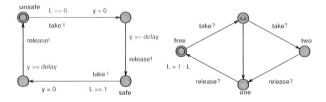

Figure 2.14: Example: The Four Vikings

Path formulae express either reachability, safety, or liveness properties. The reachability property that some state satisfying a given state formula ϕ is expressed by E<> ϕ. The safety properties that a state formula ϕ is always true is expressed by A[] ϕ, whereas A[] ϕ says that there exists a path where ϕ is always true. The classical liveness property that something good will eventually happen is expressed by A<> ϕ. Additionally, there exists a *leads to* or *response* property ϕ --> ψ, which expresses that whenever ϕ is satisfied, ψ will eventually be satisfied.

Uppaal Example

An example for a UPPAAL model taken from the demo models included in the free UPPAAL distribution is the riddle of the four vikings. The riddle is as follows: four vikings want to cross a bridge at night, but they have got only one torch and the bridge can only carry two of them. Thus, they can only cross the bridge in pairs and one has to bring the torch back to the other side before the next pair can cross. The vikings have different speeds, the fastest needs 5 minutes, the slowest 25 minutes, and the other two 10 and 20 minutes. The question is whether it is possible that all the vikings cross the bridge within 60 minutes.

To model this problem in UPPAAL, we need two timed automata templates, one for the vikings which is instantiated with the different delays, and one for the torch, see Figure 2.14. The representation of timed automata is a usual automata representation with locations connected by edges. In addition, we have two channels take and release, which model the interaction between the vikings and the torch. Furthermore, we have a data variable L which serves as a semaphore to ensure that the torch can only be on one side of the bridge at a time, and we have a clock variable y and a clock constraint $y \geq delay$ which models the time it takes the vikings to cross the bridge. A viking is on the other side of the bridge if it is in its *safe* location.

The question if they all can cross the bridge in 60 minutes can be formalized as an existential quantification over a state where all vikings are in their *safe* location and time is less or equal than 60 minutes:

E<> V1.safe ∧ V2.safe ∧ V3.safe ∧ V4.safe ∧ time ≤ 60

Note that the example of the four vikings is comparable to the question if a packet can reach its receiver in a given time limit in a communication network.

2.6 Summary

In this section, we presented the relevant background for our approach. To this end, we gave an introduction to HW/SW co-design and co-verification, in particular to some verification and validation techniques that are commonly used in HW/SW co-design. Finally, we presented the system level design language SystemC that is widely used for modeling and simulation in HW/SW co-design of digital systems, and the formal language of UPPAAL timed automata, which comes with a tool suite for modeling, simulation and animation of timed automata and a model checker.

3 Related Work

The spectrum of related work in the area of HW/SW co-verification is very broad. However, most of the existing work is non-formal and based on co-simulation and testing. For example, the SystemC Verification Standard [SCV] provides features for transaction-based test bench development, for example data introspection, randomized data generation, and callback mechanisms to observe activities at transaction level during simulation. All of these mechanism ease the development of test benches, but do neither provide support for formal specification or verification, nor for automated conformance evaluation. Similarly, in SystemVerilog [Acc03], the only supported co-verification technique is through the use of assertions, which are checked during the execution of a given design.

Only few attempts have been made to apply formal verification methods to HW/SW co-designs. In the following two sections, we first elaborate related work on formal verification for SystemC, and then related work from the area of automated test generation and conformance testing.

3.1 Formal Verification of SystemC Designs

The formal verification of SystemC designs was mainly propelled by Große et al. [DG02, GD04, GD05, GKD05, GKD06] and by Kroening et al. [KCY03, KC04, KS05, BKS08, BK08]. Große et al. focus on SystemC designs on the gate level, i. e., hardware models, and apply typical hardware verification techniques like bounded model checking and satisfiability solving. The work of Kroening et al. targets mixed hardware/software systems and uses counter-example guided abstraction refinement to enable efficient handling of both parts of a given design. In the following, we briefly present both approaches and discuss their scopes and limitations.

Formal Semantics for SystemC

There have been several approaches to give SystemC a formal semantics. A definition of the simulation semantics based on abstract state machines is given by Müller et al. [MRR03] and Ruf et al. [RHG$^+$01]. The purpose of their work is to provide a precise description of the SystemC scheduler. However, the system design itself, as built from modules, processes and channels, is not covered and therefore cannot be verified with this approach. Salem [Sal03] presented a denotational semantics for the SystemC scheduler and for SystemC processes, but only for a synchronous subset. Habibi et al. [HT05, HMT06] proposed program transformations from SystemC into equivalent state machines. In these approaches, time is ignored, and the transformation is performed manually. Besides, the state machine models do not reflect the structure of the underlying SystemC designs. Traulsen et al. [TCMM07] proposed a mapping from SystemC to PROMELA, but they only handle SystemC designs at transaction level, do not model the non-deterministic scheduler and cannot cope with primitive channels. Zhang et al. [ZVM07] introduced the formalism of *SystemC waiting-state automata*. Those SystemC waiting-state automata are supposed to allow a formal representation of SystemC designs at the delta-cycle level. However, the approach is limited to the modeling of delta-cycles, the scheduler and complex interactions between processes are not considered and the formal model has to be specified manually. Man [Man05] presented the formal language SystemC$^{\mathbb{FL}}$, which is based on process algebras and defines the semantics of SystemC processes by means of structural operational semantics style deduction rules. SystemC$^{\mathbb{FL}}$ does not take dynamic sensitivity into account, and considers only simple communications. The concept of channels is neglected. A tool to automatically transform SystemC to SystemC$^{\mathbb{FL}}$ is presented by Man et al. [MFM$^+$07]. However, it does not handle any kind of interaction between processes. Karlsson et al. [KEP06] verify SystemC designs using a petri-net based representation. This introduces a huge overhead because interactions between subnets can only be modeled by introducing additional subnets.

With our approach to define a formal semantics for SystemC, we can handle the most relevant SystemC language elements, including process execution, interactions between processes, dynamic sensitivity and timing behavior. The informally defined behavior and the structure of SystemC designs are completely preserved. The mapping from SystemC designs into UPPAAL timed automata is fully automated, introduces a negligible overhead, produces compact and comparably small models and enables the use of the UPPAAL model checker and tool suite.

Checkers for SystemC Designs

There has been some work on checkers for SystemC designs. For example, an approach to check temporal assertions for SystemC has been presented by Ruf et al. [RHaR01]. More related to our work is the work of Drechsler, Große and Kühne [DG02, GD04, GD05, GKD05, GKD06]. In [DG02], they describe how to convert a gate-level model given in SystemC into BDDs. The BDD is used for forward reachability analysis. In [GD04], they present a method which allows checking of temporal properties for circuits and systems described in SystemC, not only during simulation. A property is translated into a synthesizable SystemC checker and embedded into the circuit description. This enables the evaluation of the properties during the simulation as well as after the fabrication of the system. In [GD05, GKD05], they present an approach to prove that a SystemC model satisfies a given property using bounded model checking and show the applicability of the approach with the co-verification of a RISC CPU implemented in SystemC. In [GKD06], they use a 3-step approach. First, they verify the functional correctness of the underlying hardware using bounded model checking. Then, they verify the HW/SW interface. This means that they verify, that each instruction through which the software can access the hardware has the specified effects on all hardware blocks involved. Finally, assembler programs are verified by constraining the instructions of the program as assumptions in the proof. In other words, the instructions of a given assembler program are translated into assumptions and the known effects on the hardware are used for the proof.

The main limitation of the work of Drechsler, Große and Kühne is that their approaches are all restricted to synchronous and cycle-accurate models on register-transfer level. As a consequence, they can, in particular, not verify models using SystemC channels, necessary for transaction-level modeling (TLM), nor can they handle dynamic or timing sensitivity. With our approach, we can handle SystemC design on low abstraction-levels as well as designs on high abstraction-levels and thus we can support the whole design-process.

Abstraction Refinement for SystemC Designs

Also closely related to our work is the work of Kroening et al. In [KCY03], an approach to check consistency of C and Verilog using bounded model checking is presented. Both the circuit and the program are unwound and translated into a bit vector equation. This formula is then checked using a SAT solver. The C program has to be sequential, purely functional code, Verilog is restricted to the subset of synchronous RTL. In [KC04], an alternative approach for the same issue based on predicate abstraction is presented. In [KS05, BKS08], a labeled Kripke structure-based semantics for SystemC is proposed and predicate abstraction techniques from these structures are used for verification. They treat every thread as a labeled Kripke structure and then define a parallel composition operator to compose the threads. Thereby, they provide a formal semantics for SystemC. They furthermore present how the labels of the Kripke structures generated per process can be used to identify hardware and software parts and to automatically partition a given system description into synchronous (hardware) and asynchronous (software) parts. This partitioning is used to simplify verification by computing an abstract model of the SystemC design. The abstract model is then used for counter-example guided abstraction refinement verification.

The approach to use abstraction techniques together with model checking is also used by Blanc et al. [BK08]. There, the authors present a novel compiler for SystemC that integrates a formal and scalable race analysis. The compiler produces a simulator that uses the race analysis information at runtime to perform partial-order reduction, thereby eliminating context switches that do not affect the result of the simulation. The static computation of the race conditions relies on the Model Checking engine of SATABS (Clarke et al. [CKSY05]), a SAT-based model checker implementing predicate abstraction.

The automatic hardware/software partitioning presented by Kroening et al. allows a very efficient formal verification of SystemC designs. However, their approach does not take either timing or signal aspects into account, and complex communication is not considered. Furthermore, the scheduler is not explicitly modeled, which could pose some difficulties on further extensions of their work. With our approach, we yield formal semantics and a verification technique that supports most relevant SystemC language elements. In contrast to the approach presented by Blanc et al. [BK08], our framework is not restricted to the verification of race conditions. With our framework for automated HW/SW co-verification for SystemC designs using timed automata, we are able to verify all kinds of safety, liveness and timing properties that can be expressed in the UPPAAL subset of CTL.

3.2 Test Generation for SystemC Designs

There also exists some work on automated test generation for SystemC. Emek et al. [EN03] presented a test generation approach that generates different schedulings of transactions. With that, different execution orders of concurrent processes can be systematically covered by a test suite. The approach is extended by randomized input generation by Nahir et al. [NZE+06]. Silva et al. [dSMAP04] presented a testbench generation tool that automatically generates testbench templates for SystemC. The tool allows the definition of constraints and coverage criteria and uses the SystemC Verification Library (SCV) for constraint-based random-test generation. Standard code coverage criteria is used to determine when test generation is finished. Coverage criteria for SystemC is also analyzed by Große et al. [GPKD08]. There, untested parts of a given SystemC designs are identified using dedicated coverage criteria. Junior et al. [JCdS07] use code coverage analysis for automatic test vector generation. A coverage flow graph is constructed, and numerical optimization is used to find input vectors that force a given path. Patel et al. [PS08] proposed a model-driven validation approach for SystemC. There, directed tests are generated from ASM models. Similarly, Bruschi et al. [BFS05] generate finite state machines (FSM) from SystemC designs by performing static analysis on the source code very much like Habibi et al. [HMT06]. The FSMs are used to generate test sequences for the system under investigation. Kirchsteiger et al. [KTS+08] proposed automatic test generation for SystemC designs based on manually specified use cases. All of these approaches focus on the test input generation problem and do not use a specification to evaluate test results automatically.

3.3 Conformance Testing using Timed Automata

There have been several approaches to generate conformance tests for real-time systems from timed automata models, and in particular to generate such tests from UPPAAL models. However, most of them either consider only a restricted subclass of the timed automata model, or they do not allow static (*offline*) test generation. Springintveld et al. [SVD01] presented an approach to generate minimal test suites with complete path coverage from timed automata models. They prove that exhaustive testing is possible for real-time systems by reducing the dense-time model to a discrete model using equivalence classes. However, the authors only consider a deterministic subclass of the timed automata model. Furthermore, the size of a complete test suites is highly exponential. Cardell-Oliver [CO00] uses a similar approach, extended by a technique called *hiding*. This technique allows an abstraction of the timed automata model in order to hide parts of the system that are not relevant with respect to the test purpose. This reduces the size of a complete test suite, but the approach still cannot cope with non-deterministic specifications. Nielsen et al. [NS01] presented a technique for the automatic generation of real-time black-box conformance tests for non-deterministic systems, but only for a determinizable subclass of timed automata specifications with restricted use of clocks, guards or clock resets. Krichen et al. [KT04] proposed an algorithm for real-time test case generation for non-deterministic systems, but it is based on an on-the-fly determinization of the specification.

There also exists some work on test generation from UPPAAL models. Hessel et al. [HLN+03, HLM+08] presented the CoVer tool. CoVer allows coverage-driven conformance test generation for UPPAAL models. The test cases are generated statically and a *relativized timed input output conformance (rtioco)* relation is used to evaluate test results. However, the approach is again restricted to deterministic timed automata models. In contrast to that, the TRON (*Testing Real-time systems ONline*) tool developed by Larsen et al. [LMN05, HLM+08] can also be applied to non-deterministic systems. However, it uses an *online* test generation algorithm and thus can not be used to generate repeatable test cases. The *rtioco* relation is used again to evaluate test results.

For conformance testing in HW/SW co-verification processes, it is vital to generate conformance tests *offline*. Particularly in the context of HW/SW co-design processes based on SystemC, it is indispensable to repeatably execute test cases on each refinement stage, and thus to ensure consistency between different abstraction levels. Furthermore, SystemC designs are inherently non-deterministic. Thus, the approaches described above are not sufficient, as they either generate test cases *online*, or they do not support non-deterministic specifications. With our approach, we can generate conformance tests for *non-deterministic* systems *offline*.

3.4 Summary

There has been a considerable amount of work in the area of HW/SW verification, and in particular on the formal verification of SystemC designs. However, all of the presented approaches have their limitations. They are either restricted to subsets of SystemC that preclude them from the application during the whole design process, or they lack formal foundation, or they require a lot of manual effort. With respect to the test generation for SystemC designs, existing approaches focus on automated input selection and do not support automated conformance evaluation. Thus, they can be ideally combined with our framework, but do not solve the problem of a continuous HW/SW co-verification process. To the best of our knowledge, a comprehensive co-verification framework that supports the whole design process of digital SystemC designs with fully automatic verification techniques and yields a high degree of reliability due to the use of formal methods does not exist. With our approach, we provide such a framework.

Another contribution of this thesis is the conformance test generation from timed automata. For this challenging task, several approaches have been presented here. However, none of those provides a technique that allows the generation of conformance tests offline and supports non-deterministic system specifications at the same time. Both is necessary for a conformance test generation technique that could be embedded in the HW/SW co-verification process. With our approach, we can generate conformance tests offline from non-deterministic specifications.

4 Quality Assurance Approach

As embedded systems are often employed in safety-critical domains, the quality assurance of such systems is crucial. In particular, the digital control components of these systems have to be verified. In HW/SW co-verification, the most popular quality assurance techniques is HW/SW co-simulation. This has the advantage to be easily applicable, but lacks reliability if applied ad hoc or unsystematically. To solve this problem, we propose a continuous, comprehensive, and formally founded quality assurance process for digital SystemC designs. We obtain such a quality assurance process by a combination of model checking and conformance testing. The SystemC development process starts with an abstract design, which is stepwise refined down to the final implementation. We propose to use model checking to verify that the abstract SystemC design meets its requirements, and to generate conformance tests to verify that refined models or the final implementation conform to the abstract model. This approach yields a formally founded, comprehensive, and automated quality assurance process that continuously and naturally supports the HW/SW co-design flow throughout the whole design process. The integration of static and dynamic techniques is a particularly promising approach, as it combines the significance of formal verification with the efficiency and convenience of testing. In the remainder of this chapter, we first present a general approach for the combination of model checking and testing, and then we describe our framework for the automated HW/SW co-verification of SystemC designs.

4.1 Combining Model Checking and Testing

Static and dynamic verification techniques have both their advantages and disadvantages. Dynamic techniques, such as simulation and testing, have the advantage to be applicable without prerequisites. Furthermore, they can be applied on all development stages, including the real implementation, as long as an executable representation exists. The major drawback is their incompleteness together with the fact that test cases are often selected ad hoc and non-systematically. As testing can be used to detect defects, but not to show their absence, it is difficult to draw conclusions from a error-free test run. We never know if the design is free from defects or if the test suite is just not

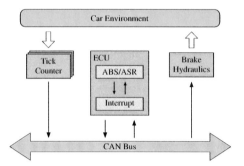

Figure 4.1: Architecture of an Anti-lock Braking System

able to detect them. In contrast to that, static techniques are complete and yield absolute guarantees about certain properties for all possible input scenarios and execution paths. Of course, this comes with a price: the effort of formal verification is much higher in terms of man power and computation time, and it can only be applied to models of the system under verification and not to the real implementation. As a prerequisite for the application of formal verification techniques, we need a formal model, which has to be manually specified by the designer or automatically generated from another model. Then, to accomplish formal verification, either a high manual effort is required if an interactive theorem prover is used, or the whole state space of a given system has to be elaborated if an automatic model checker is applied. This is particularly expensive for concurrent designs due to the combinatorial state space explosion problem. To overcome the problems that each of both kinds of verification techniques carries along, we propose to take the best of both worlds by applying formal verification in early development stages and conformance testing throughout the remaining design flow.

As a starting point, we assume a HW/SW co-development process that starts with an abstract model and refines this model down to the final implementation. This corresponds to the transaction level modeling (TLM) approach (cf. Section 2.1.2) and is common in HW/SW co-design. As an example, consider the development of a typical application from the automotive domain, an Anti-lock Braking System (ABS). An ABS monitors the speed at each wheel and regulates the brake pressure in order to prevent wheel lockup and improve the driver's control over the car. It consists of dedicated wheel speed sensors, a hydraulic modulator to control the brake pressure, an electronic control unit that runs the control algorithm, and a CAN bus that yields a fault-tolerant communication platform to connect the distributed components. An exemplary architecture of such a design is shown in Figure 4.1.

The typical HW/SW co-design flow for the development of such an ABS starts with an abstract design where processes communicate over *first in first out* (FIFO) channels and where timing is only coarsely estimated. This abstract model allows the validation and verification of the control algorithm

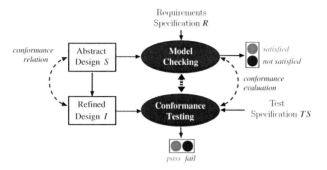

Figure 4.2: Combining Model Checking and Testing

without coping with the high complexity of the complete system, in particular by abstracting from communication, data and timing details. Then, the design is step-wise refined. For example, a high-speed CAN bus could be used for communication and an interrupt layer could be added to the electronic control unit. When these refinements are conducted, this requires detailed data and timing information. For example, modeling the CAN bus requires to refine the previously exchanged abstract transactions into bit- and cycle-accurate transactions, where each frame is transferred bit-wise in realistic transmission times.

In general, a refined design can be regarded as the implementation of an abstract design, whereas the abstract design serves as the specification. We propose to use model checking to verify that the abstract model meets its requirements. As the abstract model is relatively small compared to the implementation, the state space explosion problem can be handled on this abstraction level. Then, we propose to generate conformance tests to verify that the refined model or implementation conforms to the abstract model. This allows fully automatic conformance evaluation and can be applied throughout the whole design process down to the final implementation. The proposed idea to obtain a continuous quality assurance process for HW/SW co-designs by a combination of model checking and testing is shown in Figure 4.2. First, we use model checking to check whether an abstract design S fulfills the requirements specification R expressed in temporal logics. This yields the result *satisfied* or *not satisfied*. When the abstract design S is manually refined into a refined design I in the next development step, we assume a conformance relation between S and I and generate conformance tests to evaluate this conformance relation for a given test suite TS. The execution of the conformance tests on the refined design yields for each test case the test verdict *pass* or the test verdict *fail*. In case of the verdict *fail*, the implementation deviates from the specification and a defect has been detected.

Applied to the example of the ABS, our quality assurance approach would start with the verification of the abstract design where concurrent processes communicate through FIFO channels. Then, we use model checking to verify safety, liveness and timing properties of such a design. These properties are expressed in temporal logics and should capture all relevant design properties, in particular safety-critical properties. Example properties for the ABS are:

- the system never deadlocks

- if the wheels tend to block, the ABS eventually intervenes

- the ABS always intervenes within a given time limit

- the wheel slip never deceeds a given limit

- if the wheel deceleration exceeds the maximally possible deceleration, brake pressure is reduced within a given time limit.

All of these properties can be verified automatically using model checking. Subsequently, conformance tests can be generated to check whether the implementation conforms to the abstract design. Of course, while model checking yields guarantees for all possible input scenarios and all possible execution paths of the abstract design, the conformance of refined designs is only shown for a certain test suite and for the paths that were eventually executed during test execution. As a consequence, test cases should be repeated several times and the test suite should be carefully chosen. A complete test suite would yield the guarantee that the system was implemented correctly, but cost inacceptable effort. A test suite that covers only a few input scenarios is not sufficient to assure the quality of the system. By choosing the size of the test suite and its coverage, the best possible trade-off between computational effort and significance of the results can be achieved.

4.2 HW/SW Co-Verification Framework VeriSTA

Based on our approach for a formally founded, comprehensive, and automated quality assurance process, we developed our framework VeriSTA (**Veri**fication of **S**ystemC designs using **T**imed **A**utomata) that puts the proposed approach into practice. The framework VeriSTA and its verification flow is shown in Figure 4.3. The aim of VeriSTA is to support the whole HW/SW co-design flow with SystemC, which consists of a sequence of refinement steps. In each development stage, we have an abstract SystemC design that is manually refined to a refined SystemC design. This is shown on the left in Figure 4.3 and is the basis for the proposed verification flow. For clarity, we only consider one development step here, but the verification techniques are meant to be repeatedly applied in each development step to yield quality assurance throughout the whole design flow.

A prerequisite for the application of both model checking and conformance test generation to SystemC designs is a formal semantics for SystemC. We achieve this by a mapping from the semantics of SystemC to the well-defined semantics of UPPAAL timed automata. Using this mapping, it is possible

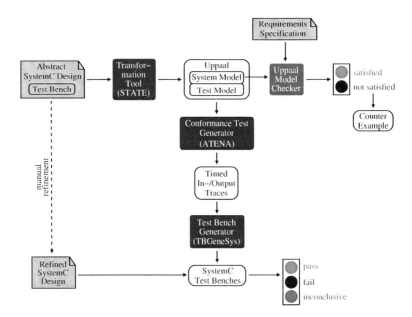

Figure 4.3: VeriSTA Framework

to translate a given SystemC design into a semantically equivalent UPPAAL model. As shown on the top of Figure 4.3, in VeriSTA the abstract SystemC design is translated into a UPPAAL model using our transformation tool STATE (SystemC to Timed Automata Transformation Engine). The resulting UPPAAL model is fed into the UPPAAL model checker, together with a requirements specification expressed in temporal logics. The model checker tries to verify that the UPPAAL model fulfills the properties defined in the requirements specification. As a result, it yields *satisfied* or *not satisfied*. If a property is not satisfied, the UPPAAL model checker additionally generates a counter-example, which can be used for debugging purposes. Note that the counter-example can also be visualized and animated in the UPPAAL tool suite. This greatly supports the designer in understanding where the problem arose from.

Model checking of SystemC designs is very expensive due to the problem of state space explosion. In particular, SystemC designs are inherently non-deterministic, since the SystemC scheduler chooses the execution order of concurrent processes non-deterministically. As a consequence, model checking can only be applied to small or abstract designs. To overcome this problem, and to be able to also cope with more detailed and comparably large designs, we propose to generate conformance tests for refined designs. Like model checking, the automatic generation of conformance tests also requires a formal model to have a precise and unique interpretation of the specification. In our VeriSTA

framework, we again use the UPPAAL model to this end. From that, we statically compute all possible timed output traces for a given test suite consisting
of a set of input traces. This is implemented in our ATENA tool (**A**utomated
Test generation **E**ngine for **N**on-deterministic Timed **A**utomata). The required test suite has to be defined by the designer as a SystemC test bench
and is translated into a UPPAAL test model as part of the abstract SystemC
design. Note that the model checker ignores the test model and verifies the
requirements for all possible input scenarios. From the set of input traces (defined by the test model) together with the timed output traces (allowed by
the specification), we generate SystemC test benches. This is implemented in
our tool TBGeneSys (**T**est **B**ench **Gen**erator for **Sys**temC). The generated
test benches can be used to execute and evaluate conformance tests fully automatically. This is achieved by monitoring the outputs of the refined SystemC
design during test execution respectively HW/SW co-simulation, and by comparing them with the timed output traces allowed by the specification. For
the comparison, we use the *relativized timed input/output conformance relation
(rtioco)* defined by Larsen et al. [LMN05]. The result of the test execution is
a test verdict, which is either *pass*, *fail*, or *inconclusive*. In case of the test
verdict *pass*, the refined design conforms to the specification according to the
used conformance relation. In case of *fail*, an error was detected. The test verdict *inconclusive* is added for the special case that the specification contains
non-terminating internal loops. In such cases, the conformance test generation
is aborted when a given limit of computation steps is exceeded and the test
verdict is *inconclusive*.

Altogether, our framework yields a fully automatic verification flow that
supports the whole HW/SW co-design process of digital HW/SW systems modeled in SystemC. However, neither the semantics-preserving transformation
from SystemC to UPPAAL timed automata, nor the automatic generation of
conformance tests for SystemC designs are trivial. In the next two chapters, we
first present the transformation, which allows the application of the UPPAAL
model checker, and then the conformance test generation method.

5 Formal Semantics for SystemC

For quality assurance, simulation is necessary but not sufficient because it is usually impossible to cover all possible input scenarios. As a consequence, defects can be defected, but it is impossible to show their absence. It requires formal verification techniques such as model checking to *guarantee* important properties, e. g., liveness, safety, and the abidance of real-time constraints, of a given system. A vital precondition to formally verify such properties is a formal semantics. Unfortunately, the semantics of SystemC is only informally defined in [IEE05]. This makes it difficult to analyze SystemC designs, and even impossible to apply automatic formal verification techniques like model checking. To solve this problem, we first present a formal semantics for SystemC. Second, we present how our formal semantics can be used to model check SystemC designs.

The general idea to obtain a formal semantics for SystemC is that we map the informally defined semantics of SystemC to the formally well-defined semantics of UPPAAL timed automata [BLL$^+$95]. To this end, we define a semantically equivalent UPPAAL representation for all relevant executable SystemC language elements, e. g., for simple assignments, method calls, events and the wait-notify mechanism. Then, we present a transformation procedure to construct a complete UPPAAL model from a given SystemC design using these representations. The overall transformation preserves the informally defined semantics of SystemC completely. To ease debugging, it also keeps the structure of the original SystemC design transparent to the designer in the UPPAAL model. Furthermore, the mapping we present allows the *automatic* generation of a formal UPPAAL model from a given SystemC design. This in turn facilitates the application of the UPPAAL model checker to SystemC designs. Note that the UPPAAL tool suite enables simulation and animation of the generated model and thus allows the visualization and animation of counter-examples if the verification fails.

In the following, we first state a few assumptions that define the subset of SystemC supported by our approach. Second, we present our general approach for the representation of SystemC in UPPAAL. Then, we present the complete transformation procedure. We conclude the chapter with an illustration of the verification flow that allows model checking of SystemC designs.

5.1 Assumptions

SystemC is a language that allows the modeling of digital hardware and software components on different levels of abstraction. To this end, SystemC supports a very diverse set of models of computation. At the same time, as an extension of C++ , it inherits the full semantic scale of the C++ language. Together, this illustrates that SystemC is an outstandingly expressive languages. To make it nonetheless possible to transform SystemC designs into the more restricted UPPAAL modeling language, we assume that a given SystemC design fulfills the following restrictions. First of all, UPPAAL supports no dynamic variable or process creation. Thus, dynamic object or process creation are also forbidden in the SystemC design, i.e., a static structure is required. This is a minor restriction because dynamic object or process creation is rarely used in the considered application domain of safety-critical embedded systems. Dynamic process creation is not even part of the SystemC language definition and can only be used through the corresponding C++ functions. Since the UPPAAL model is statically composed at transformation time, all statements that are used for instantiation and binding must be evaluable at transformation time. As a consequence, only instantiations and initializations are allowed in constructors and in the sc_main method. This again is an unimportant restriction. While SystemC allows hierarchical scopes, the possibility to define scopes is limited to global and local variables in UPPAAL. To avoid name conflicts, we assume that no variables are shadowed (i.e., each variable has a unique identifier in its scope). Similarly, we assume that no overloading of methods is used. These are assumptions that do not restrict the set of possible input designs but requires some renaming and code duplication at the most. Finally, the UPPAAL modeling language only provides the data types int and bool. Most complex data types can be mapped to integers, but the use of pointers is generally impossible in UPPAAL. Thus, we assume that the SystemC design does not use any pointers. As a consequence, dynamic memory management is also excluded. Again, this is non-essential, as dynamic memory management is rarely used in the considered application. Overall, the assumptions on the input SystemC design hardly narrow the applicability of our approach and are fully acceptable in the considered domain of digital control systems that are often safety-critical.

5.2 Representation of SystemC Designs in Uppaal

Figure 5.1 shows how we represent SystemC designs in UPPAAL. The general idea is that each method is mapped to a single timed automata template. Process automata are used to encapsulate these methods and care for the interactions with events and the scheduler. The scheduler is explicitly modeled, and we use a predefined template for events and other SystemC constructs such as primitive channels. The interactions between the processes and the scheduler are modeled by two synchronization channels, *activate* and *deactivate*. The interactions between processes and event objects are modeled by

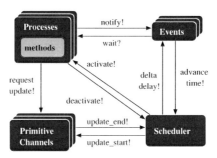

Figure 5.1: Representation of SystemC Designs in UPPAAL

wait and *notify*. The interactions between the event objects and the scheduler are used to synchronize their timing. The scheduler informs the event objects when a delta-cycle is completed to release delta-delay notifications, and conversely, the event objects inform the scheduler when time is advanced due to a timed notification.

To allow compositional transformation, that is to make it possible that each SystemC module can be translated separately, we perform the mapping from SystemC to UPPAAL in three steps:

(i)   We define a (general) timed automata representation for each SystemC language construct, such as methods, processes, and events.

(ii) Using these general representations, we translate each given SystemC module into a set of parameterized timed automata.

(iii) We perform instantiation and binding. This requires to instantiate the parameterized timed automata, to add the variables and channels that are necessary to connect them, and to build the system declaration.

Note that with the help of the template parameters, we can instantiate the modules an arbitrary number of times without having to perform a new translation. When we compose a design, we instantiate the modules including their events and processes and connect them using synchronization channels. Using this compositional approach, we are able to translate large designs in reasonable time. The generated models are structure-preserving and thus easily comprehensible to the designer. We can handle all relevant SystemC language elements, including process execution, interactions, dynamic sensitivity and timing behavior. In the following sections, we first outline a few assumptions we pose on the input SystemC design to make sure that it can be completely transformed into a semantically equivalent UPPAAL model. Then, we present the transformation of all important SystemC language constructs and show how a design is composed using instantiation and binding.

5.3 Design Transformation

In this section, we describe how we map SystemC language elements to timed automata representations and how these mappings are embedded in the complete design transformation. The transformation preserves the (informally defined) behavioral semantics and the structure of a given SystemC design. It can be applied fully automatically and the resulting models can directly be fed into a model checker. In the following, we first present the transformation of sequential control flow, i. e., methods and regular C/C++ statements. Second, we describe the transformation of the SystemC elements that allow the modeling of concurrent processes and their interactions, i. e., the scheduler, processes, events and time. Third, we describe how the structural elements, i. e., channels and modules, are transformed. Finally, we present how a design is composed by instantiation and binding.

5.3.1 Method Transformation

The basic building blocks to structure sequential code are methods. They contain all executable statements and thus constitute the executable part of the design. In our transformation approach, methods are translated into timed automata templates, which are then embedded in process automata that care for the interaction with events and the scheduler. This allows the independent and separate transformation of methods.

Methods contain lists of statements. Our general transformation procedure for a method is as follows: Initially, we generate an empty timed automata template, the only location is the initial location. We append a transition labeled with a synchronization that can be used to transfer control flow to the method, and a target location for this transition. This location is the starting point for the executable statements contained in the method. Then, we process the method statement by statement, and for each statement, we append locations and transitions labeled with the corresponding actions. When we reach the end of the method, we append a transition that leads back to the initial location and transfers control flow back to the caller.

The transformation of methods is shown in Figure 5.2. The SystemC code of a method declaration and the corresponding method call is shown in Figure 5.2a, the resulting UPPAAL elements are shown in Figure 5.2b and Figure 5.2c. A method transfers the control flow from the *caller* to the *callee*. The *callee* executes the *method body* and returns the control flow back to the caller. To model call-return semantics, we use a synchronization channel ctrl. The caller, depicted in Figure 5.2c, hands control over to the callee, depicted in Figure 5.2b, with ctrl!. Then, the caller waits until the method body of the callee is executed, and resumes execution when receiving ctrl?. The method template waits for ctrl? in its initial location and executes its method body when it receives the ctrl signal. Then, it executes its method body and sends ctrl! back to the caller. For the transfer of arguments to a method, dedi-

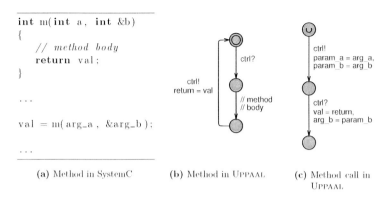

Figure 5.2: Method Transformation

cated global variables `param_p` for each parameter p of a method are declared. Figure 5.2 illustrates how two arguments `arg_a` and `arg_b` are passed to the method. The first argument `arg_a` is passed *by value*, and thus its value is copied into the variable `param_a`. The second argument `arg_b` is passed *by reference*. Thus, its value is copied into the variable `param_b` before the method execution *and* back to `arg_b` afterwards. Similarly, a return value is transferred from the method to the caller using a dedicated variable `return`. The control transfer channel and the input and output parameters of a method are visible as parameters of the timed automata templates of the method and the caller. This enables multiple instantiations of a method and the connection with different callers in the system declaration. Local variables of a method are adopted as local variables of the template.

In the following, we describe which locations and transitions have to be appended for each kind of statement. The statements can be of type *method call, return, assignment, if-else, switch-case, while, continue* or *break*. We use the term *current location* to refer to the lastly appended location in each transformation step. We also keep a reference to the initial location, and to the beginning of blocks. Note that time may only pass within a method if a `wait` function is called or if the control flow is passed to another method that possibly calls a `wait` function. As a consequence, we use *urgent* locations in all other cases. Non-urgent locations are only used when a method waits for a synchronization. This ensures the correct timing behavior of methods.

Return statement If we reach a ***return*** statement, we connect the current location with the initial location and label this transition with `ctrl!` and possibly with the assignment of the return value as shown in Figure 5.2. A return statement aborts the transformation of the current block, and subsequent statements are dead code.

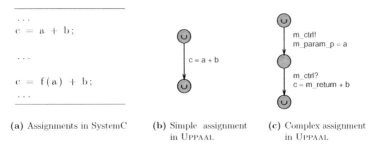

(a) Assignments in SystemC   (b) Simple assignment   (c) Complex assignment
                              in Uppaal   in Uppaal

Figure 5.3: Assignment Transformation

Assignment transformation We adopt *assignments* as *updates* at transitions in the timed automata template. An assignment may contain arithmetic operations and method calls. Arithmetic expressions in SystemC are syntactically equivalent to those in Uppaal, as Uppaal supports *updates* in C notation. Thus, they can be adopted without further handling. If an assignment contains a method call, the method call is transformed first as described above, and its return value is used where the method is called. For the transformation of an assignment, we make the current location urgent, append a transition with the assignment as *update* label, and use a new location as target location. An example is shown in Figure 5.3. In Figure 5.3a, two assignments, a simple arithmetic expression and a complex assignment including a method call are shown. The corresponding representations in Uppaal are shown in Figure 5.3b and Figure 5.3c.

If-else transformation To transform *if-else* statements, we append two outgoing edges to the *current location* as shown in Figure 5.4, one of them labeled with the if-condition, the other with the negated if-condition. Again, we make the current location urgent because the evaluation of the if-condition takes no time. We recursively transform all statements of the then-block and append them to the if-location. We also transform the statements of the else-block and append them to the else-location. If there is no return statement in both branches, they are joined in a new location which becomes the current location. If there is a return statement in one of the branches, it is connected to the initial location and execution of the method is finished for this branch. In that case, we use the last node of the other branch as new current location. If there are return statements in both branches, transformation of the current block is finished.

Switch-case transformation A *switch-case* statement allows a case differentiation dependent on a switch expression that evaluates to an integer value. For the transformation of a *switch* statement, the switch expression is first evaluated and stored in a temporary variable. Then, for each switch case, two

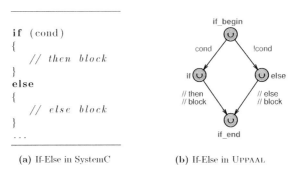

```
if (cond)
{
    // then block
}
else
{
    // else block
}
...
```

(a) If-Else in SystemC   (b) If-Else in UPPAAL

Figure 5.4: If-Else Transformation

edges are appended to the current location. The first one is labeled with the condition for the current case, the other one with the negated condition for the current case. Then, the statements of the current case are appended to the first transition, and the next switch case to the latter. If the conditions are false for all cases, an optional default case is executed. In all cases, a *break* statement is translated to an edge to the end of the switch statement. If a switch case does not contain a *break* statement, the following case is executed without checking its condition. An example for the transformation of a *switch-case* statement is illustrated in Figure 5.5.

Loop transformation   The transformation of loops is depicted in Figure 5.6. Figure 5.6b shows the transformation of a *while loop*, Figure 5.6c the trans-

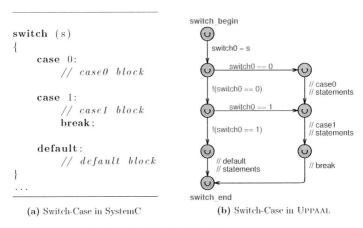

```
switch (s)
{
    case 0:
        // case0 block

    case 1:
        // case1 block
        break;

    default:
        // default block
}
...
```

(a) Switch-Case in SystemC   (b) Switch-Case in UPPAAL

Figure 5.5: Switch-Case Transformation

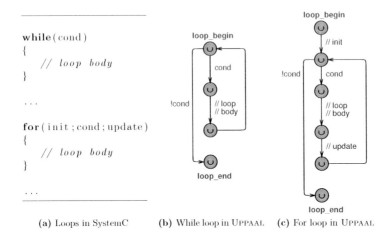

(a) Loops in SystemC   **(b)** While loop in UPPAAL   **(c)** For loop in UPPAAL

Figure 5.6: Loop Transformation

formation of a *for loop*. The conditions are transformed similar to those of *if-else* statements. The transition that leads into the loop is guarded by the condition itself, the other by its negation. The loop body is transformed and appended to the location reached by the fulfilled condition. When the loop body is completely executed the condition is checked again and if it evaluates to false, the loop is left, if it evaluates to true the loop body is executed again. A *for-loop* is equivalent to a *while-loop*, but additionally contain an initialization part and an update part. The initialization part is executed before the condition is firstly checked, the update part is executed at the end of each execution of the loop body. For *return* statements, the current location is connected with the initial location, as described above, and the execution of the loop is therefore aborted. Within a loop, the *continue* statement can be used to abort the current execution of the loop body, and the *break* statement can be used to abort the execution of the loop completely. As a consequence, if we have a *continue* statement, we connect the current location with the location *loop_begin*, i. e., the loop is executed from the beginning if the loop condition is still fulfilled. For a *break* statement, we connect it with the location *loop_end*, i. e., the loop is left in any case.

In this subsection, we presented all transformations that are necessary to transform methods, i. e., sequential control flow. Note that all of these transformations can be applied independently without knowledge about the surrounding system structure. This makes the whole transformation approach modular, flexible, and easily extensible. In the next subsections, we present the more sophisticated and more specific SystemC language constructs that allow a discrete-event simulation of concurrent processes and the modeling of time.

5.3.2 Concurrency and Communication

SystemC events are executed in a discrete event-simulation, and the semantics of SystemC is defined by the simulation semantics. The heart of the simulation is the SystemC scheduler, which allows the concurrent execution of SystemC processes. In this subsection, we present the transformation of the SystemC elements that allow the modeling of concurrent processes and their interactions, i. e., the scheduler, processes and events.

The Scheduler

The scheduler controls the execution of SystemC designs. The basic execution units are processes. The simulation semantics of SystemC is described in Section 2.4.3. The scheduler works in delta-cycles, i. e., in evaluate and update phases. In the evaluate phase, processes that are *ready to run* are executed in non-deterministic order. In the update phase, primitive channels are updated by taking over new values. If there are no more processes *ready to run* when a delta-cycle is finished, time is advanced to the next pending event.

The timed automaton we use to model the scheduler is shown in Figure 5.7. Initialization is implicit in UPPAAL, i. e., processes and methods are executed once before the main simulation loop. As a consequence, the scheduler starts in the evaluation phase depicted by the location `evaluate`. If there are any processes that are *ready to run*, the scheduler sends an activation event `activate!`. Processes that are *ready to run* receive this event and resume their execution. We use a binary channel for the activation to ensure that only one process is executed at a time and that processes are executed in a non-deterministic order. To ensure that the scheduler sends the activation event once for each process that is *ready to run*, each process increments a counter `ready_procs` when triggered, and decrements the counter when suspending itself. When

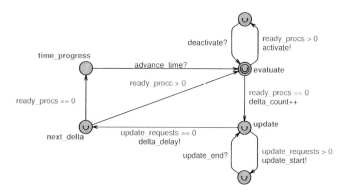

Figure 5.7: Timed Automaton modeling the Scheduler

there are no more processes that are *ready to run*, i.e., `ready_procs == 0`, the scheduler starts the update phase by going to location `update`. In the update phase, *update requests* are executed in non-deterministic order using the activation event *update_start*. Immediate notification is not allowed during the update phase. If there are no more update requests, the scheduler starts the next delta-cycle (see location `next_delta`). When leaving the update phase, the scheduler informs event objects with pending *delta-delay notifications* that a delta-cycle is finished by sending `delta_delay!`. If there are delta-delay notifications, the corresponding processes are immediately triggered and become *ready to run*. They will be executed in the next delta-cycle, which is started by the scheduler without time progress. If there are no processes triggered by *delta-delay notifications*, i.e., `ready_procs == 0`, simulation time must be advanced to the earliest pending timed notification. There are two types of timed notifications in SystemC: events may be notified with a delay by calling `e.notify(t)`, and processes may be delayed for a given time interval by calling `wait(t)`. In SystemC, the timing behavior is completely managed by the scheduler. In the timed automaton, we have the possibility to wait locally for a given time. Therefore, it is more suitable to model time within processes and event objects. To wait for the earliest pending timed notification in the scheduler, we let the processes and events with timed behavior send a broadcast synchronization `advance_time!` when their delay expires. The scheduler receives `advance_time?` and starts a new delta-cycle, i.e., executes processes that became ready to run through the *timed notification*.

The timed automaton modeling the scheduler behaves exactly like the SystemC scheduler. The binary channels used to control process execution and channel updates guarantee that the model checker considers every possible serialization. The locations used for the execution of delta-cycles are urgent and thus take no simulation time. We ensure that no scheduling phase is started before the preceding phase is completed using the counters `ready_procs` and `update_procs` and committed locations in event notifications. The counters guarantee that pending executions are completed before the next phase is started. The use of committed locations in event notification (as shown in the next section) ensures that event triggering is prioritized over state changes in the scheduler.

Events

If an event object `e` is notified by its owner, processes that are sensitive to the event resume execution. SystemC supports three types of event notifications. An *immediate notification*, invoked by `e.notify()`, causes processes to be triggered immediately in the current delta cycle. A *delta-delay notification*, invoked by `e.notify(0)`, causes processes to be triggered at the same time instant, but after updating primitive channels, i.e., in the next delta-cycle. A *timed notification*, invoked by `e.notify(t)` with `t > 0`, causes processes to be triggered after a certain delay `t`. If an event is notified that already has a pending notification, only the notification with the earliest expiration time takes effect. That means that immediate notifications override all pending

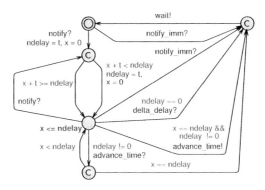

Figure 5.8: Timed Automata Template for an Event Object

notifications, delta-delay notifications override timed notifications, and timed notifications override pending timed notifications if their delay expires earlier.

We model event objects as shown in Figure 5.8. The timed automata template is instantiated for each event object declared in a given SystemC design. Its template parameters are the synchronization channels `notify_imm`, `notify` and `wait`, and the integer variable t. Initially, the event just waits to be notified. If it is immediately notified, it receives `notify_imm?`, and immediately sends `wait!` on a broadcast channel. If the event object is notified by a delta-delay or a timed notification, it receives `notify?` and copies the parameter t to a local variable `ndelay`, which yields the notification delay. At the same time, a local clock x is reset. The committed location that is now reached is used to reinitialize `ndelay` and to reset x if a subsequent delta-delay or timed notification overrides the notification delay. We then have to wait until:

(i) an immediate notification overrides the current pending notification,

(ii) we receive `delta_delay?` from the scheduler if `ndelay == 0`, or

(iii) the current delay expires, i.e., `x == ndelay && ndelay != 0`.

Subsequently, we send `wait!` and go back to the initial location. When a timed notification expires, we have to inform the scheduler to start the next evaluation phase by sending `advance_time!`. Due to the use of a broadcast channel `advance_time!`, only the first `advance_time` is received by the scheduler if the delays of multiple events expire at the same time. As mentioned before, the preservation of the SystemC semantics requires that the scheduler must not start the evaluation phase before event notification is completed. To ensure this, event objects with pending timed notification also synchronize with `advance_time?` as receivers. If they receive `advance_time?` and their delay expires in the same time instant, i.e., if `x == ndelay`, they immediately trigger pending processes. Otherwise, nothing happens. The semantics

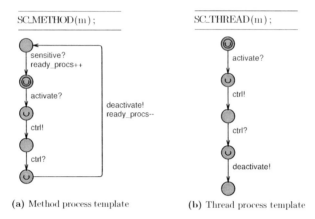

(a) Method process template   (b) Thread process template

Figure 5.9: Process Templates

of broadcast synchronization ensures that events with expiring delays reach the committed location in the same semantic step as the scheduler reaches the evaluation phase. The committed location ensures that events are prioritized in the next semantic step.

Processes

Processes are the basic execution unit in SystemC. Each process is associated with a method to be executed. There are two types of processes: *method processes* and *thread processes*. A *method process*, when triggered, always executes its method body from the beginning to the end. It is triggered by a set of events given in a static sensitivity list. The timed automata template we use to wrap a method process is in Figure 5.9a. It waits for any of the events from the sensitivity list by synchronizing on *sensitive?*. If one of the events from the sensitivity list occurs, it marks itself as *ready to run* by incrementing *ready_procs* and by waiting for the *activate* event. Then, it transfers control to its associated method. When the method returns, it deactivates itself by sending *deactivate!* to the scheduler and by decrementing *ready_procs*. Then, it returns to the initial position and waits until it is triggered by one of the events from the sensitivity list again. A *thread process* may suspend its execution and dynamically wait for events or a given time delay. It is triggered only once at the beginning of the simulation and runs autonomously from that time on. The timed automata template we use to start a thread process is given in Figure 5.9b. It just waits to be activated, transfers control flow to its associated method and deactivates itself if the method returns. Note that the control transfer channel is a parameter of the process templates, and thus the same template can be instantiated for arbitrary many process declarations.

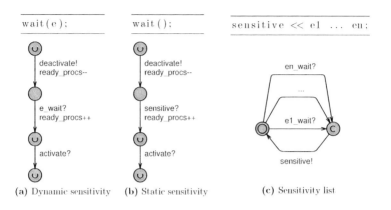

(a) Dynamic sensitivity   (b) Static sensitivity   (c) Sensitivity list

Figure 5.10: Event Sensitivity

Static and dynamic sensitivity

SystemC designs are executed in a discrete-event simulation. This means that concurrent processes are triggered by events at discrete times. A process that listens to an event, i.e., waits for it to be triggered, is called *sensitive* to this event. A process may be sensitive to multiple events at a time. In the following, we describe how we model processes and their static and dynamic sensitivity A *thread process* may suspend its execution by calling a *wait* function. If wait() is called without parameters, it waits for one of the events in the static sensitivity list. If the process calls wait(e) with an event e as argument, the static sensitivity list is temporarily overridden by e. This is called *dynamic sensitivity*. If the process calls wait(t), it is delayed by t time units. If the process calls wait(t,e), it waits for event e for t time units. We model event sensitivity in UPPAAL using synchronization channels as shown in Figure 5.10.

Dynamic sensitivity   A process calling wait(e) is shown in Figure 5.10a. It suspends its execution, i.e., it synchronizes with deactivate!, decrements a counter ready_procs, and then waits to be triggered, i.e., it synchronizes with the wait channel of the event object. When e_wait? is received, the process increments the counter ready_procs and waits to be activated by the scheduler. We can also handle waiting for composed events such as e1 & e2 or e1 | e2.

Static sensitivity   Static sensitivity is very similar to dynamic sensitivity, but when wait() is called the process waits for one of the statically known events from the sensitivity list. We model sensitivity lists by a timed automaton, which waits for one of the specified events and sends sensitive! on a broadcast channel if one of them occurs, as shown in Figure 5.10c. To ensure

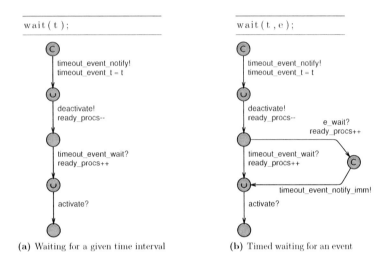

(a) Waiting for a given time interval   (b) Timed waiting for an event

Figure 5.11: Timed Waiting

that immediate event notifications take effect immediately, we use a committed location. Figure 5.10b illustrates how we model static sensitivity within a sensitive process. Compared to dynamic sensitivity, e_wait? is replaced by sensitive?.

Timed waiting We model timed waiting with a special timeout_event. Each process has its own timeout_event. Calls to wait(t) are modeled as shown in Figure 5.11a. First, a timed notification is released to start the timeout. Second, the process waits for the timeout to expire by synchronizing with timeout_event_wait?. Waiting for an event until a timing delay expires (wait(t,e)) requires to extend the timed automata model by a synchronization on e_wait?, as shown in Figure 5.11b. To make sure that a timeout_event does not override subsequent timed notifications, we override it with an immediate event notification if event e occurs.

5.3.3 Channels and Modules

Channels and modules define the structure of a SystemC design. Channels define communication methods which may be used by processes, whose modules are connected to them through ports.

Channels We transform the communication methods defined within a channel like ordinary methods as described above. The communication methods are connected to processes, which have access to the channel in the instantiation and binding phase using the UPPAAL template mechanism. The overall channel is transformed in the same way as a module. A special treatment is required for primitive channels, because they support the *request-update* mechanism. Primitive channels have to implement an `update()`-function. This is called by the special function `request_update()` in the evaluation phase if a communication method wants the `update()`-function to be executed in the update phase. We use a timed automata template to manage update requests as shown in Figure 5.12. If `request_update?` is received, the `update` method of the corresponding channel is called within the update phase of the scheduler. Calls to `request_update()` in SystemC are modeled by sending `request_update!` in the timed automata template. The execution of the `update` method is performed by the scheduler as described above.

Modules   The transformation of a module or channel requires that we adopt the member variables as global variables, allocate synchronization channels and parameter declarations, and generate the necessary method templates. All of these elements are prefixed with the module name to make the structure of the original SystemC design transparent in the generated UPPAAL model. A module or channel may be instantiated multiple times in a SystemC design. To make method templates reusable, we take all declarations that are visible in the module as template parameters. When a module or channel is transformed, the corresponding templates are generated. Global and system declarations are not added to the UPPAAL model until a module or channel is instantiated.

5.3.4   Instantiation and Binding

In the instantiation and binding phase, all generated UPPAAL elements are composed into the final system. To this end, the method templates generated from modules and channels are instantiated and connected through their parameters. Event and process templates are generated once for each module or channel. Methods, however, may be used in multiple concurrent processes. Therefore, all methods that are visible to a module must be instantiated once for each process declared within the module. The corresponding global dec-

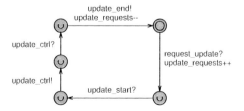

Figure 5.12: Timed Automata Template for Request-Update

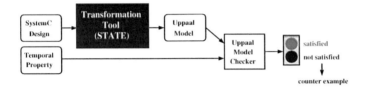

Figure 5.13: Verification Flow with STATE

larations are prefixed with the module name and the process name. Member
methods of channels must be instantiated once for each process of each module
which is bound to the channel.

Although there is no structural hierarchy in UPPAAL, the module structure of the SystemC design is visible through prefixes. In combination with
a one-to-one mapping of SystemC to UPPAAL processes, the design structure
is completely transparent to the designer. This is very useful when the model
checker produces counter-examples.

5.4 Model Checking SystemC Designs

We presented an approach to translate SystemC designs into the UPPAAL
timed automata, whose semantics is well-defined. The translation enables the
usage of the UPPAAL tool suite on SystemC designs, including the UPPAAL
model checker to formally verify temporal properties of SystemC designs.

The main advantage of our approach is that once we have defined the
mapping from SystemC to UPPAAL, the transformation of a given SystemC
design can be performed automatically. We implemented this in our STATE
(SystemC to Timed Automata Transformation Engine) tool. This transformation tool makes it possible to verify temporal properties of SystemC designs
fully automatically. The automated verification flow is shown in Figure 5.13.
The STATE tool takes as input a SystemC design and a temporal property
formulated in the UPPAAL requirement language (which is a subset of CTL).
The SystemC design is translated into a UPPAAL model by our STATE tool
and can then be directly passed to the UPPAAL model checker. The model
checker tries to verify the property and generates a counter-example if it is
not satisfied. Note that the counter-example is given as a trace in UPPAAL
semantics. However, the transformation from SystemC to UPPAAL preserves
the structure by prefixing, such that it is transparent to the SystemC designer
where the problem arises from. In addition, UPPAAL can be used to animate
the counter-example graphically.

6 Conformance Testing

The aim of conformance test generation is to compute all possible output traces of a high-level specification for a given set of input traces and to use these output traces to automatically evaluate the conformance of a low-level implementation. In our case, we want to generate conformance tests from a high-level SystemC design and to use them to evaluate low-level SystemC designs or the final implementation. To this end, the high-level SystemC design is first automatically translated into a UPPAAL timed automata model. From the UPPAAL model, we compute all possible output traces for each of the given input traces. From each input trace together with its corresponding set of possible output traces, we generate a SystemC test bench. The resulting set of SystemC test benches can be used for automatic conformance evaluation of low-level designs.

The automatic generation of conformance tests requires a clear definition of both the semantics of the specification, from which the tests are generated, and the *conformance* relation that is used for test evaluation. To this end, we present a complete definition of the symbolic semantics of UPPAAL timed automata, and give a formal definition of *relativized timed input/output conformance relation*. Based on these definitions, we present an efficient algorithm for the computation of all possible output traces of a UPPAAL model for a given input trace. Finally, we present how a SystemC test bench for automated conformance evaluation can be automatically generated from a given input trace together with the corresponding set of possible output traces. Altogether, we obtain a framework that allows fully automatic conformance evaluation in a HW/SW co-design flow with SystemC. The framework is applicable to non-deterministic systems and conformance tests are generated offline. With that, it is ideally suited to support a HW/SW co-design flow where the SystemC design is stepwise refined down to the final implementation. In such a design flow, the conformance tests can repeatedly be executed in each development phase. Thus, they can be used to ensure the consistency between the designs on different abstraction levels.[1]

---

[1] Note that the execution of the generated test benches requires the points of control and observation, i. e., the interface between the test bench and the system under test, to be of the same type on different abstraction levels. Otherwise, adapters may be required

In the following sections, we first describe the basic test setting that we require to make our conformance testing approach applicable. Then, in Section 6.2, we give a complete definition of the symbolic semantics for UPPAAL timed automata, and define the conformance relation in Section 6.3. In Section 6.4, we present our algorithm for the computation of all possible output traces for a given UPPAAL model. In Section 6.5, we describe how we generate SystemC test benches from that.

6.1 Test Setting

Embedded systems closely interact with a technical environment. Because of that, both SystemC designs and UPPAAL models comprise an explicit model of the environment in addition to the system model. The environment model provides the inputs to the system model and consumes its outputs. A test case can be regarded as a specialized environment that provides a single input trace. It is specified as a timed automaton that sends input events and data at certain times and waits for system reactions for a given amount of time. A particular location indicates the end of the input trace and can be used by the test algorithm to terminate the state space exploration. We call the automaton that provides the input trace a *test automaton*. Note that a SystemC input generator that provides a single input trace can be automatically transformed into such a test automaton.

On the output side, we want to observe all possible behavior the specification could produce. Thus, we need an environment that accepts all possible outputs at arbitrary times. To this end, we use a *generic tester* component that accepts all possible responses as proposed by Robinson-Mallett et al. [RMHL06]. Like the test automaton, the generic tester can also be generated automatically from a corresponding SystemC output monitor.[2] Together, the test automaton and the generic tester constitute a test model that replaces the environment model in the UPPAAL model used for the test generation process, as shown in Figure 6.1.

From the test model together with the system model, conformance tests are generated. The resulting test benches still contain the test automaton, but the generic tester is replaced by an automaton that accepts exactly those traces that were produced by the abstract system model or specification for the given input trace. We call this automaton a *checker automaton*. If the checker automaton reaches its final node during test execution, it received a complete and correct output trace and the test verdict is *pass*. If it receives an unexpected event, unexpected variable values or a clock bound is exceeded, the test verdict is *fail*. If it receives a trace for which the correct output trace could not be completely computed, the test verdict is *inconclusive*. In the

---

to translate, for example, a bit-accurate frame into an abstract data type before the generated test bench can be used for automated conformance evaluation.

[2]As an output monitor must exist to make a SystemC design executable, it usually already exists.

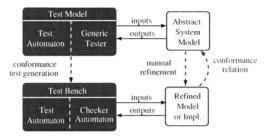

Figure 6.1: Conformance Test Generation

following sections, we describe how such checker automata can be generated automatically.

6.2 Symbolic Semantics of Uppaal Timed Automata

The first step to generate conformance tests from UPPAAL timed automata is to compute the possible behavior of the model for a given input trace. To that end, we have to explore the symbolic state space that is reachable with the given input trace. As a prerequisite for that, we need a complete definition of the symbolic semantics of UPPAAL timed automata. The symbolic UPPAAL semantics is described by Bengtsson et al. [BY04]. However, the description is incomplete. The extension of networks of timed automata with shared data variables is only implicitly described, and binary and broadcast channels are omitted. In the following, we give a complete symbolic semantics of UPPAAL timed automata.

A network of UPPAAL timed automata is a transition system where symbolic states are triples $\langle \bar{l}, D, v \rangle$ with

- a location vector $\bar{l}$,

- a difference bound matrix D representing a clock zone,

- a vector of data variable evaluations v.

As UPPAAL provides the template mechanism to instantiate one automata definition multiple times in a system, we use the term process to denote a concrete automaton in the system. We further define the following abbreviations:

- $I_c(l)$, $I_v(l)$ denote the invariants assigned to location l, w.r.t. to clock resp. data variables,

- $I_c(\bar{l})$, $I_v(\bar{l})$ denote the conjunction of all invariants assigned to locations in $\bar{l}$,

- $D^\uparrow$ denotes the operation $\mathbf{up}(\mathbf{D})$, i.e., removes upper bounds of all clock variables,

- $\mathscr{U}(\bar{l})$ is the set of urgent locations in $\bar{l}$,

- $\mathscr{C}(\bar{l})$ is the set of committed locations in $\bar{l}$,

- g_{ic}, g_{iv} denote guards on clocks resp. data variables, as an abbreviation we use $g_i = (g_{ic}, g_{iv})$,

- r_{ic}, r_{iv} are sets of update operations on clock resp. data variables,

- $u(D, r_{ic})$, $u(v, r_{iv})$ denote the application of update operations on a clock zone resp. the global data space, as an abbreviation we use $r_i = (r_{ic}, r_{iv})$,

- $c!$, $c?$ denote sending and receiving on a synchronization channel c.

Initially, all clocks are set to zero and all processes are in their initial location.

Definition 12 (Symbolic semantics of UPPAAL networks of timed automata). *A* UPPAAL *network of timed automata (UTA) consists of n processes $\mathscr{A}_i = (L_i, l_i^0, C, A, E_i, I_i)$ and a global data space consisting of a set of variables V. The symbolic semantics of UTA is defined by a transition system $(S, s_0, \rightarrow)$. Each state $s \in S$ is a tuple $(\bar{l}, D, v)$, where $\bar{l}$ is a location vector, D is a clock zone and v a vector of variable values. A semantic step can be either*

(i) a time step *or* delay,

(ii) an independent step of a single process *or* internal transition,

(iii) a binary synchronization *between two processes, or*

(iv) a broadcast synchronization *between one sender process and k of receiver processes.*

Delay A *delay* is a semantic step where the UTA stays in the same locations and all variable values remain unchanged. Only the difference bound matrix (DBM) representing the clock zone is changed by first removing upper bounds and then intersecting with the conjunctive invariant of all current locations. In other words, a delay denotes the expansion of the current clock zone to the upper limit given by the invariants of the current locations. A delay is only admissible if none of the locations of the current state is urgent or committed.

$$\langle \bar{l}, D, v \rangle \rightsquigarrow \langle \bar{l}, D', v \rangle$$
$$\text{with} \quad D' = D^\uparrow \wedge I_c(\bar{l})$$
$$\text{if}$$
$$\mathscr{U}(\bar{l}) = \emptyset \wedge \mathscr{C}(\bar{l}) = \emptyset$$

Internal transition An *internal transition* is an independent transition of a single process i. As effect of the transition, the location of this process l_i

is replaced by a successor location l_i' in the location vector, and the action assigned to the corresponding edge is performed. This may include an update of the variable vector $u(v, r_{iv})$ and operations on clocks $u(D, r_{ic})$. An internal transition is only admissible if the guard assigned to the edge is satisfied and if the invariant of the successor location is not violated. To obtain the clock zone where both conditions are fulfilled, the DBM is first conjuncted with the guard, then possible clock operations are performed and, finally, the DBM is conjuncted with the invariant. If the resulting DBM is non-empty, it represents the clock zone of the successor state. An internal transition is only admissible if the corresponding process is in a committed location or if the set of committed locations is empty.

$$\langle \bar{l}, D, v \rangle \rightsquigarrow \langle \bar{l}', D', v' \rangle$$
$$\text{with} \quad \bar{l}' = \bar{l}[l_i'/l_i], D' = u(D \wedge g_{ic}, r_{ic}) \wedge I_c(\bar{l}'), v' = u(v, r_{iv})$$
$$\text{if}$$
$$l_i \xrightarrow{g_i, \tau, r_i} l_i'$$
$$D \in g_{ic} \wedge v \in g_{iv},$$
$$D' \neq \emptyset \wedge v' \in I_v(\bar{l}'),$$
$$(l_i \in \mathscr{C}(\bar{l}) \vee \mathscr{C}(\bar{l}) = \emptyset)$$

Binary synchronization A *binary synchronization* is a conjoint transition of two processes i and j that synchronize on the same binary channel c with i as sender and j as receiver. As effect of a binary synchronization, the locations of both processes are replaced by a successor location in the location vector and the actions assigned to the corresponding edges are performed. Note that the actions assigned to the sender's edge are performed first, and only then, the actions assigned to the receiver's edge are performed on the resulting data and clock variables. Guards and invariants are used similar to an internal transition, the only difference is that both guards and invariants have to be considered. A binary synchronization is only admissible if one of the processes is in a committed location or if the set of committed locations is empty.

$$\langle \bar{l}, D, v \rangle \rightsquigarrow \langle \bar{l}', D', v' \rangle$$
$$\text{with} \quad \bar{l}' = \bar{l}[l_i'/l_i, l_j'/l_j], D' = u(u(D \wedge g_{ic} \wedge g_{jc}, r_{ic}), r_{cj}) \wedge I_c(\bar{l}'),$$
$$v' = u(u(v, r_{iv}), r_{jv}))$$
$$\text{if}$$
$$l_i \xrightarrow{g_i, c!, r_i} l_i' \wedge l_j \xrightarrow{g_j, c?, r_j} l_j'$$
$$D \in (g_{ic} \wedge g_{jc}), v \in g_{iv} \wedge v \in g_{jv},$$
$$D' \neq \emptyset \wedge v' \in I_v(\bar{l}')\rangle,$$
$$(l_i \in \mathscr{C}(\bar{l}) \vee l_j \in \mathscr{C}(\bar{l}) \vee \mathscr{C}(\bar{l}) = \emptyset)$$

Broadcast synchronization A broadcast synchronization is a conjoint transition of one sender i with all currently enabled k receivers $j = j_1, ..., j_k$. The effect is similar to that of a binary transition, all locations of participating processes are replaced by a successor location in the location vector and the actions assigned to the corresponding edges are performed. To determine the order of these actions, the order of the processes in the system declaration is used and all actions are performed successively. All guards and invariants of participating processes have to be considered for the effect on the clock zone and to determine admissibility of the synchronization. Furthermore, a broadcast synchronization is only admissible if one of the processes is in a committed location or if the set of committed locations is empty.

$$\langle \bar{l}, D \rangle \rightsquigarrow \langle \bar{l}', D', v' \rangle$$
$$\text{with} \quad \bar{l}' = \bar{l}[l_i'/l_i, l_{j_1}'/l_{j_1}, ..., l_{j_k}'/l_{j_k}],$$
$$D' = u(u(D \wedge g_{ic}, r_{ic}) \wedge (\wedge g_{jc}), \bigcup r_{jc}) \wedge I_c(\bar{l}'),$$
$$v' = u(u(v, r_{iv}), \bigcup r_{jv})$$
$$\text{if}$$
$$l_i \xrightarrow{g_i, c!, r_i} l_i' \wedge l_{j_1} \xrightarrow{g_{j_1}, c?, r_{j_1}} l_{j_1}' \wedge ... \wedge l_{j_k} \xrightarrow{g_{j_k}, c?, r_{j_k}} l_{j_k}'$$
$$D \in \wedge(g_{jc}) \wedge v \in \wedge(g_{jv}),$$
$$D' \neq \emptyset \wedge v' \in I_v(\bar{l}'),$$
$$(l_i \in \mathscr{C}(\bar{l}) \vee (\exists l_j \in \mathscr{C}(\bar{l})) \vee \mathscr{C}(\bar{l}) = \emptyset)$$

A **deadlock** occurs when there is no successor state for a given state. If one or more of the guards of outgoing transitions split a given symbolic state, the existence of successor states must be checked for each sub-zone.

With the above definitions, we have a clear and unique definition of the behavior of a UPPAAL timed automata model and can compute all possible behavior from a given model. Before we describe our algorithm for conformance test generation, we present the conformance relation we use for automated conformance evaluation.

6.3 Conformance Relation

The aim of conformance testing is to determine whether an implementation of a system conforms to its specification. This requires to define precisely what it means that an implementation *conforms* to its specification. For that, a formal *implementation* or *conformance relation* is used [Tre96]. A *conformance relation* relates an implementation with its specification. In our case, both the implementation and the specification are SystemC designs and can be described by *timed labeled transition systems* with inputs and outputs. As a consequence, we can use the *relativized timed input/output conformance (rtioco)* relation defined by Larsen et al. [LMN05, HLM+08]. The *rtioco* relation was defined for UPPAAL timed automata and thus is ideally suited for our test setting where we derive conformance tests from a UPPAAL model.

A prerequisite to relate an implementation to a specification is that the implementation can be modeled by some formal object (cf. Section 2.3.3). However, an implementation is usually a non-formal object. To solve this problem, Bernot [Ber91] introduced the concept of a *test hypothesis*. Following that, it is sufficient to assume that an implementation could hypothetically represented by some formal model. In our case, we assume that the low-level design (or at least its observable behavior) could hypothetically be transformed into a semantically equivalent UPPAAL model. With that, we can define timed traces, a refinement relation on timed traces, and finally the *relativized timed input/output conformance relation* with respect to UPPAAL timed automata models and use it for the conformance evaluation of SystemC designs.

In Section 2.5, we introduced symbolic timed traces for timed automata networks without data variables as sequences of actions and clock zones. For timed automata networks with data variables, an action may be composed of an event e and a manipulation of the global data space v. As a consequence, when the system state changes, we can observe either an event e, a modified data space v, or both. As we are only interested in the *observable behavior*, we partition both the events and the data space into three disjoint sets of input events/variables Ev_{in}/V_{in}, output events/variables Ev_{out}/V_{out}, and internal events/variables Ev_{int}/V_{int}. With that, a *timed input or output trace* can be defined as follows:

Definition 13 (Timed input and output traces). *A timed input (output) trace of a state s is a (possibly infinite) sequence of observations, where each observation is a tuple (e,D,v) consisting of an event $e \in Ev_{in}$ ($e \in Ev_{out}$), a difference bound matrix D representing the clock zone in which the event occurs, and a vector $v \in V_{in}$ ($v \in V_{out}$) containing the values of data variables that are externally visible as inputs (outputs) at this time.*

$$ttr_{i/o}(s) = (e_0,D_0,v_0)(e_1,D_1,v_1)...(e_i,D_i,v_i)...$$

Based on the definition of timed input and output traces, we can define the *refinement relation* $\leq$ on timed output traces:

Definition 14 (Refinement relation on timed output traces). *A timed output trace o_I refines a timed output trace o_S if they contain the same events and variable values, and if the clock zone of each observation on I is a subset of the corresponding observation on S. We use the index set I over the elements of o_I and o_S.*

$$o_I \leq o_S \quad \text{iff} \quad \forall i \in I : o_I^i.e = o_S^i.e \wedge o_I^i.D \subseteq o_S^i.D \wedge o_I^i.v = o_S^i.v$$

Note that the number of elements in o_I and o_S may be finite or infinite. If the number of elements is finite for one of the timed output traces, $o_I \leq o_S$ if and only if $length(o_I) = length(o_S)$.

The set of timed output traces that can be observed on a system S under environmental constraints $\mathscr{E}$ for a given input trace σ are denoted by

TTr$_o$$((I,\mathscr{E}),\sigma)$. The set of timed input traces that are provided by an environment are denoted by TTr$_i(\mathscr{E})$.

Definition 15 (Refinement relation on sets of timed output traces). *We define the refinement relation $\sqsubseteq$ on sets of timed output traces with respect to a given environment $\mathscr{E}$ such that for each output trace of the implementation o_I an output trace of the specification o_S with $o_I \leq o_S$ must exist:*

$$TTr_o((I,\mathscr{E}),\sigma) \sqsubseteq TTr_o((S,\mathscr{E}),\sigma) \quad iff$$
$$\forall o_I \in TTr_o((I,\mathscr{E}),\sigma) : (\exists o_S \in TTr_o((S,\mathscr{E}),\sigma) : o_I \leq o_S)$$

Based on the definition of timed traces and the refinement on sets of timed output traces, we can define *relativized timed input/output conformance (rtioco)* as follows:

Definition 16 (Relativized timed input/output conformance (rtioco)). *I conforms to S under the environmental constraints $\mathscr{E}$ if for all timed input traces $\sigma \in TTr_i(\mathscr{E})$ the set of timed output traces of I is a refinement of the set of timed output traces of S for the same input trace.*

$$I \ rtioco \ S \quad iff \quad \forall \sigma \in TTr_i(\mathscr{E}) : TTr_o((I,\mathscr{E}),\sigma) \sqsubseteq TTr_o((S,\mathscr{E}),\sigma)$$

The *rtioco* relation is derived from the *input/output conformance (ioco)* relation of Tretmans and de Vries [dVT00] by taking time and environment constraints into account. Under the assumption of weak input enabledness, i. e., if any input is accepted in any state, the *rtioco* coincides with timed trace inclusion. Note that the definition ensures that the implementation may not produce outputs that are unexpected by the specification and that it must produce outputs whenever it is expected by the specification.

Together, the symbolic UPPAAL semantics and the conformance relation yield the formal basis for our conformance test approach. With the above definitions of timed output traces, refinement on timed output traces and conformance between an implementation and its specification, we can use the following procedure to check whether a given implementation conforms to its specification based on the observable behavior:

(i)   compute all possible timed output traces of the specification for a given timed input trace,

(ii) execute the implementation for the same timed input trace,

(iii) check whether the timed output trace of the implementation refines the set of timed output traces allowed by the specification by comparing output events, clock zones, and variable assignments.

In the following section, we first present an algorithm for the first task, i. e., for the computation of all possible timed output traces of the specification for a given timed input trace. Then, we present how SystemC test benches can be generated from that. These test benches allow both the execution of a given implementation and for the automated conformance evaluation, i. e., they fulfill the second and the third task.

6.4 Conformance Test Generation

To generate conformance tests from a given UPPAAL timed automata model and a given input trace, we have to explore the complete symbolic state space that is reachable with the given input trace. To this end, the algorithm for test generation explores the state space breadth-first until the end of the given input trace or a deadlock state is reached. Central in the algorithm is the computation of all possible successor states for a given symbolic semantic state following the symbolic semantics of UPPAAL timed automata. In the following, we first describe a basic algorithm for *offline* test generation. Then, we present how all possible successor states of a given symbolic semantic state are computed within this algorithm. Finally, we describe extensions and optimizations to make the algorithm efficient with respect to time and memory consumption.

6.4.1 Basic Algorithm

The aim of the algorithm for conformance test generation is to compute all possible output traces from a given UPPAAL timed automata model for a given input trace. Note that in our case, the input trace is part of the given UPPAAL model. To compute the state space that is reachable with that input trace, we perform a breadth-first search. This means that we start with the initial symbolic state $(\bar{l}, D, V)$ consisting of a location vector $\bar{l}$, a difference bound matrix D representing a clock zone, and a set of global variables V. From that, we compute all possible successors. Then, we compute all possible successor states for each of the successors and so forth, until we reach the end of the input trace specified in the test automaton (*end* location).

The overall algorithm is shown in Listing 6.1. It operates on a UPPAAL network of timed automata. From that, it builds two state sets: The WAIT set is used to store all states for which the successors are not computed yet, the KNOWN set is used to store states that are completely processed, i. e., for which all successor states are computed. The set STATESPACE is used to store the so far explored state space, i. e., it holds tuples of states and their successor states. As long as the WAIT set is non-empty, states are taken from it. If the selected state is neither a deadlock state nor contains an end location and the limit of computation steps is not exceeded, the successor states are computed. For each of the successors, we check whether we have already visited it. If not, we add it to the WAIT set. When all successor states of a state are computed, it is added to the KNOWN set. The algorithm terminates when the end of the test case or a deadlock state is reached. The result is a tree of all possible computation paths for a given timed input trace. To get the observable behavior, we just have

```
WAIT  := { ⟨l̄₀,D₀,V₀⟩ } ;
KNOWN := ∅ ;
STATESPACE := ∅ ;
while WAIT ≠ ∅ do
   select  s = ⟨l̄ₛ,Dₛ,Vₛ⟩  from  WAIT;
   if  !isEnd(s)  and  !isDeadlock(s)  and  !limitExceeded(s)
      successors :=  getSuccessors(s);
      for  each  successor ∈ successors
         if  successor ∉ (KNOWN ∪ WAIT)  then
            add  successor  to  WAIT;
         end  if
      end  for
   end  if
   add  ⟨s,successors⟩  to  STATESPACE;
   add  s  to  KNOWN;
end  while
return  getOutputs(STATESPACE);
```

Listing 6.1: Test Generation Algorithm

to extract the outputs from the computation tree, including the corresponding difference bound matrices and externally visible data valuations.

As the system may be non-deterministic, the result of the algorithm shown in Listing 6.1 is a tree, where each path represents a possible timed output trace. By joining all its end states into a final node *pass*, as shown in Figure 6.2, the tree can be transformed into a checker automaton as described in Section 6.1. Note that we limit the number of internal computation steps between two output events to ensure termination of the algorithm in case of infinite internal loops. If the limit is exceeded, the corresponding node in the checker automaton is marked with the label *inconclusive*. If the checker au-

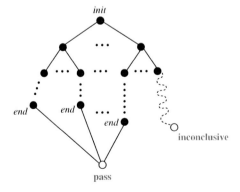

Figure 6.2: Checker Automaton

tomaton reaches this node, the verdict is *inconclusive*. That means that the test generation algorithm was not able to predict the correct behavior for the given input trace together with the previous observations. A *fail* node is not explicitly contained in the checker automaton. The test verdict is *fail* whenever something unexpected happens.

6.4.2 Computation of Successor States

The heart of the test generation algorithm shown in Listing 6.1 is the *get-Successors* function, which determines all possible successor states of a given state. This function implements the symbolic semantics of UPPAAL timed automata and considers all four kinds of symbolic semantic steps that are defined in Section 6.2. A precondition for that is to determine which semantic steps are possible from a given state.

The first kind of a symbolic semantic step, i. e., a delay, is possible whenever there are no urgent or committed locations in the location vector of the current state. It is performed by expanding the clock zone to the maximum that is allowed by the current invariants. We do this at first, to ensure that we use the maximal clock zone for the following determination of possible discrete steps.

To obtain all possible discrete steps, we first determine all enabled outgoing edges from the current location vector. An edge is enabled, if its guard is satisfied. The possible internal transitions can be directly derived from the set of enabled edges. The possible synchronizations depend on the number of possible communication partners. Remember that in the case of more than two communication partners for a binary transition, actual partners are non-deterministically chosen. For the computation of all possible successor states, that means that every possible combination has to be considered. The same holds if there is a non-deterministic branch between multiple sending or receiving edges in one process. As a consequence, we have to compute all possible sets of communication partners for each channel. As an example, consider the three automata shown in Figure 6.3. The automaton shown in Figure 6.3a synchronizes as a sender on a broadcast channel c. The automata shown in Figure 6.3b and Figure 6.3c synchronize as receivers. As both receivers implement a non-deterministic choice between two branches, the sender can synchronize with edge 1 of both receivers, with edge 2 of both receivers, or with edge 1 of one of the receivers and edge 2 of the other receiver. In other words, each combination has to be considered to obtain the set of enabled synchronizations.

The required steps to compute all possible successor states of a given state can be summarized as follows:

(i) collect all outgoing edges and all edges with urgent or committed source locations (initialization),

(ii) expand the current clock zone to the maximally possible *delay*,

(iii) build the set of enabled edges,

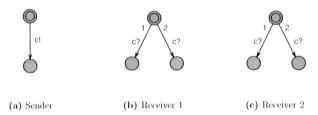

(a) Sender   (b) Receiver 1   (c) Receiver 2

Figure 6.3: Communication Partners of a Broadcast Synchronization

(iv) from the set of enabled synchronization edges, build the sets of possible communication partners,

(v) compute all successor states that are reachable by an *internal transition*, a *binary synchronization*, or a *broadcast synchronization*.

In the following, we describe these steps in more detail. Altogether, they constitute an algorithm for the computation of all possible successor states for a given symbolic semantic state.

Initialization The initialization phase, where outgoing edges and all edges with urgent or committed source locations are collected, is shown in Listing 6.2. The algorithm takes a symbolic state $\langle \bar{l}, D, v \rangle$ as input. From that, it builds the set of outgoing edges OUT, the set of edges with committed source locations COMMIT, and the set of edges with urgent source locations URGENT. Furthermore, the sets INTERNAL, SYNC, and SUCCESSORS are used to store the set of internal edges, the set of synchronizing edges, and the set of successor states, respectively. Initially, those sets are empty.

Delay The first semantic step performed on the input state is a *delay*. This ensures that the clock zone of s is expanded to the maximum, before we compute possible successor states. The delay(s) function used in Listing 6.3

```
s := ⟨l̄, D, v⟩ ;
OUT := outgoingEdges(l̄) ;
COMMIT := committedEdges(l̄) ;
URGENT := urgentEdges(l̄) ;
INTERNAL := ∅ ;
SYNC := ∅ ;
SUCCESSORS := ∅ ;
```

Listing 6.2: Initialization

```
if COMMIT = ∅ and URGENT = ∅ then
  s := delay(s);
end if
```

Listing 6.3: Semantic Step: Delay

implements the *delay* as defined in Section 6.2, i.e., it expands the current clock zone as far as the invariants of the current locations permit. A delay is only possible if both the set of committed and the set of urgent locations are empty.

Determine Enabled Edges In the next step, we build the set of enabled edges as shown in Listing 6.4. If the COMMIT set is non-empty, only internal edges with committed source locations may be enabled. An edge is internal if it has no *synchronization* label and enabled if its guard is satisfied. In addition to the set of enabled internal edges, we need to compute the set of enabled synchronization edges. A synchronization edge is enabled if its guard is satisfied. Which synchronizations are enabled can not be determined until all potential communication partners are known. To prepare the computation of all possible sets of communication partners for each channel, we collect enabled channels together with its potential senders and receivers in a channel set CHAN.

Determine Enabled Synchronizations The set of possible binary and broadcast synchronizations depends on the set of enabled synchronization edges. How we determine all possible combinations of communication partners to compute the set of enabled synchronizations is shown in Listing 6.5. In the case of binary synchronizations, one sender synchronizes with one receiver. If there are more than two possible communication partners, the UPPAAL semantics prescribes that pairs are non-deterministically chosen. For the computation of the set of all possible successor states, this means that all possible pairs have to be considered. As a consequence, we have to iterate over all receivers and combine them with all senders that are not from the same process. If the COMMIT set is non-empty, we have to take care that only pairs are chosen where one of communication partners is in a committed location. In the case of broadcast synchronizations, each sender synchronizes with all currently enabled receivers that are not from the sender process. Care has to be taken to avoid that two receivers from the same process are taken. If there are multiple receivers from the same process, a synchronization is enabled for each alternative. The set of enabled synchronizations is stored in the SYNC set.

Execute Discrete Semantic Steps The final step in the computation of all possible successor states for a given state is to execute all possible discrete semantic steps. As we have identified all enabled edges and enabled synchronizations, we just have to perform the corresponding operations as described

```
(* if there are committed edges, only those may be enabled *)
if COMMIT ≠ ∅ then
 EDGES := COMMIT
else
 EDGES := OUT
end if

(* edges are enabled if their guard is satisfied *)
for each edge ∈ EDGES
  if edge has no sync then
    if guard(edge) is satisfied then
      add edge to INTERNAL;
    end if
  end if
end for

(* initialize active channel set *)
CHAN := ∅

(* collect all enabled synchronization edges *)
for each edge ∈ OUT
  if edge has sync then
    if guard(edge) is satisfied then
      if channel(edge) ∉ CHAN
        add channel(edge) to CHAN;
      end if
      if edge is sender then
        add edge to sender list of channel(edge);
      end if
      if edge is receiver then
        add edge to receiver list of channel(edge);
      end if
    end if
  end if
end for
```

Listing 6.4: Determine Enabled Edges

```
for each channel ∈ CHAN
  if COMMIT = ∅ or (channel has receiver or sender ∈ COMMIT)
    for each sender of channel
      if channel is broadcast
        RECV := get receivers from channel with
                      process(receiver) ≠ process(sender);
        PREV_RECV_SETS := {∅};
        for each proc ∈ PROCESSES
          PREV_RECV_SETS_NEW := ∅;
          PROC_RECV := get receivers from RECV with
                          process(receiver) = proc;
          (* append each receiver of the current process
             to each previously computed receiver set *)
          for each RECV_SET ∈ PREV_RECV_SETS
            for each proc_recv ∈ PROC_RECV
              add RECV_SET ∪ {proc_recv} to PREV_RECV_SETS_NEW;
            end for
          end for
          (* keep new list of receiver sets *)
          PREV_RECV_SETS := PREV_RECV_SETS_NEW;
        end for
        for each SYNC_RECV ∈ PREV_RECV_SETS
          if COMMIT = ∅ or
             sender ∈ COMMIT or
             SYNC_RECV ∩ COMMIT ≠ ∅
            add ⟨sender, SYNC_RECV⟩ to SYNC;
          end if
        end for
      else (* binary channel *)
        for each receiver of channel
          if process(receiver) ≠ process(sender) then
            if COMMIT = ∅ or sender ∈ COMMIT or receiver ∈ COMMIT
              add ⟨sender, {receiver}⟩ to SYNC;
            end if
          end if
        end for
      end if
    end for
  end if
end for
```

Listing 6.5: Determine Enabled Synchronizations

```
for each edge ∈ INTERNAL
   compute ⟨l′,D′,v′⟩;
   if D ≠ ∅ then
      add (τ,⟨l′,D′,v′⟩) to SUCCESSORS;
   end if
end for

for each sync ∈ SYNC
   compute ⟨l′,D′,v′⟩;
   if D ≠ ∅ then
      add (sync,⟨l′,D′,v′⟩) to SUCCESSORS;
   end if
end for
```

Listing 6.6: Execution of All Possible Discrete Semantic Steps

in Section 6.2, i. e., to replace the source with the target locations, to perform the actions assigned to the edges, and to constrain the clock zone according to the guards and invariants of the target locations. Note that we check whether the resulting clock zone is non-empty before we add successor states to the SUCCESSORS set. With that, we ensure that we do not add states that violate an invariant.

Overall, we presented an algorithm with which all possible symbolic successor states for a given symbolic state can be computed. Together with the algorithm shown in Listing 6.1, we have a complete algorithm to generate conformance tests from a given UPPAAL model. However, although the presented algorithm is fully operative, it leaves room for optimizations, which we present in the following section.

6.4.3 Optimizations

The problem with the basic algorithm shown in Listing 6.1 is that it suffers from the same state space explosion problem as model checking. The computation is limited by the size of the input trace. Still, the non-deterministic behavior of the SystemC scheduler leads to an explosion of semantic states in the partial computation tree, which must be fully explored for the given input trace to obtain all possible output traces. A well-established mean to reduce the number of semantic states in a computation tree is to recognize semantic states that have already been explored before. The disadvantage of this technique is that it requires to keep all states in the memory. This blows up the memory usage and finally is the reason why large models cannot be handled by standard model checkers. The main idea of our optimized algorithm for conformance test generation is to make use of the specifics of the SystemC semantics to drastically reduce the number of semantic states that have to be kept in memory during state space exploration. To this end, we make use of SystemC delta-cycles, the cooperative scheduler, and linear time progression.

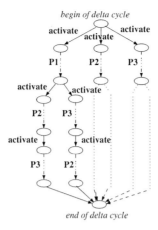

Figure 6.4: Non-deterministic Process Execution

Whenever we realize that we do not need to keep a set of states for further computations, we can write the corresponding trace information out (to hard disk), and delete it from the main memory. This reduces the computational effort significantly and mitigates the *out of memory* problem considerably.

The primary source of non-determinism in SystemC designs is the scheduler semantics, which executes concurrent processes in non-deterministic order within a **delta-cycle**. However, in most cases, e.g., in the case of primitive channels using the request-update scheme, the result is still uniquely determined. In our partial computation scheme, this means that at the entry point of a delta-cycle, we have many branches due to the non-deterministic scheduler behavior. However, if the program behavior is uniquely determined, all of these branches lead to the same semantic state at the end of the delta-cycle. An example is shown in Figure 6.4. At the beginning of the delta-cycle, one of three processes is non-deterministically chosen. After that, one of the others is chosen. In any case all three processes have been executed at the end of the delta-cycle and the same semantic state is reached (i.e., the resulting observable behavior is uniquely determined). The first optimization of the basic algorithm is to recognize such behavior and to delete all intermediate semantic states from memory if all semantic states in a delta-cycle have a common and unique successor state. This can be efficiently checked because we can identify the states at the beginning and at the end of a delta-cycle. If we reach the state at the end of a delta-cycle, we just have to check whether all states that are successors of the state at the beginning of the delta-cycle are also predecessors of its end state.

Another possibility to reduce the state space explosion is to remove intermediate states in processes. As SystemC uses a **cooperative scheduler**, process execution always consists of a sequence of non-preemptive execution steps. Since we can never start a process between non-preemptive statements, we can delete all semantic states between a process activation and its deactivation from memory. Care must be taken if the designer implemented infinite loops without preemption. This is generally unwanted behavior because it starves all other processes in the design. However, we can recognize such behavior and ensure termination of the test generation algorithm. To this end, we detect cycles between process activation and deactivation. If we detect such a cycle, we abort test case generation and give a corresponding error message.

Altogether, the presented optimizations, which make use of delta-cycles and the cooperative scheduler semantics, reduce the memory consumption and the computational effort significantly. In addition to that, we extended the algorithm for conformance test generation by hashing, by a memory efficient representation of the difference bound matrix, and by a strategy to store states in swap files whenever the available heap space falls below a given limit. This potentially increases computation time but solves the *out of memory* problem and makes the approach applicable to all kind of models that are supported by the transformation approach, given that enough computation time is spent and that sufficient hard drive space is available.

6.5 Test Bench Generation

In this section, we present how we generate SystemC test benches for automated conformance evaluation from the previously computed set of expected output traces. To this end, a checker automaton is constructed, which accepts the expected outputs at the expected times and yields the test verdict *pass* if a correct output trace is completely received, the test verdict *inconclusive* if an output trace could not be completely computed, and the test verdict *fail* otherwise. The main challenges for the generation of SystemC test benches from such checker automata are to cope with output ports providing only blocking read access, and to ensure that time limit exceedings are recognized.

The generated test benches consist of the originally used input generator and an automatically generated monitor module, which reads the outputs of the design under test, checks their correctness, and yields the test verdict. To this end, all output channels of the design under test are used as inputs to the monitor module. The structure of the automatically generated monitor module is shown in Figure 6.5.

For the correctness check, a look-up-table (LUT) is constructed from the previously computed possible output traces. It contains expected variable values $(v_0, ..., v_n)$, lower and upper bounds on the global clock (g_l, g_u), and possible successor states $(s'_0, ..., s'_m)$ for each semantic state s. Thus, each entry of the LUT has the following form:

$$lut(s) = \langle (v_0, ..., v_n), (g_l, g_u), (s'_0, ..., s'_m) \rangle$$

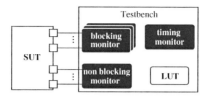

Figure 6.5: Structure of Automatically Generated Monitor Modules

Within the monitor module, a member variable is used to hold the current state. Note that a state in the monitor module is not equivalent to the semantic state of the design under test, because we hide all variable and clock assignments that are not visible to the environment. Thus, the LUT contains only observable variable assignments and the global clock.

The output ports of a given SystemC design may provide *blocking* or *non-blocking* read functions. If a port provides only non-blocking read functions, a process reading from these ports is blocked as long as nothing happens on the port. For non-blocking ports, the reading of the outputs of a given design under test consists of a sequence of read functions. In the case of blocking ports, we have to take care that the test verdict of the monitor module does

```
SC_METHOD(monitor_nb)
sensitive << i1 << i2 << ... << in;
...
void monitor_nb() {
  bool verdict = false;
  int locVars[n];

  locVars[0] = i1.read();
  ...
  locVars[n-1] = in.read();

  if(inconclusive(s)) verdict = inconclusive;

  if(locVars == vars(s)) verdict = true;

  for(s' : succ(s))
    if(locVars == vars(s')) {
      s = s'; change.notify();
      verdict = true;
    }

  if(!verdict) verdict = fail;
}
```

Figure 6.6: Generated Monitor for Non-Blocking Read Functions

```
SC_THREAD(monitor_time)
...
void monitor_time() {
  sc_time now;
  while(true) {
    lb = lower_bound(s); ub = upper_bound(s);
    now = sc_time_stamp();
    if(lb > now || now > ub) // test verdict fail
    wait(ub - now, SC_NS, change);
    if(sc_time_stamp() > ub) // test verdict fail}
} }
```

Figure 6.7: Generated Timing Monitor

not depend on the order of events. We solve this problem by using multiple monitor processes. One thread process is generated for each input port that provides blocking read access. Each of them contains a blocking read call and subsequently uses the LUT to check whether a correct input was received. Additionally, one method process is generated that is sensitive to all input ports that provide non-blocking read access. Whenever triggered, this process also uses the LUT to check whether a correct input was read. The general structure of a method process that observes non-blocking ports is shown in Figure 6.6. The thread processes that observe blocking ports are constructed very similar, the only difference is that they have no static sensitivity list and that they read only from one port each. In both cases, a correct input is received if one of the expected successor states of the current state is reached or if the system could still be in the current state. If the actual variable assignments do not match to those of the current state or one of the successor states, test execution is aborted and the test verdict is *fail*. All monitor processes notify a *change* event whenever they change the current state. As there are multiple processes controlling the current state in case of output channels that provide blocking read access, the monitor processes allow the preserving of variable assignments of the current state instead of reaching one of the successor states. To control the timing, a timing monitor thread is generated as shown in Figure 6.7. This thread reads the lower and upper bounds on the global clock from the LUT on every change event and uses a `wait` statement with timeout to ensure that the state is changed at the correct time. If the state change event occurs too early or too late, test execution is aborted and the test verdict is *fail*.

6.6 Automated Conformance Evaluation

In this chapter, we presented an approach for the automated evaluation of the conformance of a low-level SystemC design to its specification. The specification is given as a UPPAAL model, which is automatically generated from a high-level SystemC design. To establish a formal basis for that, we first presented a complete definition of the symbolic UPPAAL semantics as well as a conformance relation that can be used to relate a SystemC implementation to a UPPAAL specification. Then, we presented an efficient algorithm to compute all possible output traces from a given UPPAAL model, and we described how SystemC test benches can be generated from those traces. These test benches can be directly executed with the low-level design under test and provide the test verdict *pass*, *fail*, or *inconclusive* for each input trace specified in the test suite. Note that our conformance evaluation approach is applicable on multiple levels of abstraction, as long as the corresponding adapters, which translate between the abstraction levels, are provided. As a consequence, it can be used for quality assurance throughout the whole design flow. As we generate the test benches for automated conformance evaluation *offline*, we can reuse them in each development step. With that, we ensure the consistency between designs on different abstraction levels with minimal computational effort. Most importantly, the whole conformance evaluation approach we presented is automatically applicable. Solely the test suite must be provided by the designer, but we are currently working on an approach for automatic input generation as well.

7 Implementation

We presented a comprehensive and automatically applicable approach for the HW/SW co-verification of SystemC designs using timed automata. The approach is put into practice with our VeriSTA framework. To evaluate its practical applicability, we implemented the complete VeriSTA framework. As shown in Figure 7.1, the VeriSTA framework consists of three main components:

- a *transformation tool* translates a given abstract SystemC design into a semantically equivalent UPPAAL model,

- a *conformance test generator* computes all possible output traces from the UPPAAL model, and

- a *test bench generator* generates SystemC test benches from that.

We implemented these components in three tools: The SystemC to Timed Automata Transformation Engine (STATE) translates a given SystemC design into a semantically-equivalent UPPAAL timed automata model. The Automated Test generation Engine for Non-deterministic Timed Automata (ATENA) computes all possible output traces from the UPPAAL model. Finally, the Test Bench Generator for SystemC (TBGeneSys) constructs a SystemC test bench from these output traces, which can be used for automated conformance evaluation. Together with the external UPPAAL model checker, these components implement the complete VeriSTA framework.

All three components are implemented in the platform independent programming language Java. They can be executed on all kinds of platform that provide a Java Virtual Machine. The complete implementation comprises about 10.000 lines of code. In the following, we summarize the main characteristics of STATE, ATENA, and TBGeneSys.

7.1 STATE

We presented how to transform a given SystemC design into a semantically equivalent UPPAAL timed automata model in Chapter 5. The transformation is modular and precisely defined and captures all relevant language constructs

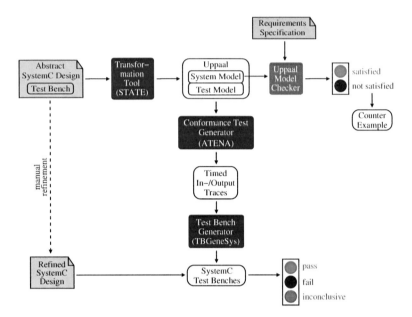

Figure 7.1: VeriSTA Framework

of SystemC. As a consequence, a given SystemC design can be automatically translated. We implemented this automatic translation in the diploma thesis of Joachim Fellmuth [Fel08]. The result is the SystemC to Timed Automata Transformation Engine (STATE).

STATE takes a SystemC design as input and yields a corresponding UP-PAAL model as output. As a front-end for SystemC, we used the *Karlsruhe SystemC Parser* (KaSCPar) [FZI]. KaSCPar parses a given SystemC design and generates an *Abstract Syntax Tree* (AST) in XML. The AST in XML serves as input for STATE, which generates a UPPAAL model that is also in XML format and that can be used as input for the UPPAAL tool suite. Figure 7.2 shows the tool chain from SystemC to UPPAAL. Within STATE, the transformation of a given SystemC design is performed in two phases: first, the *transformation engine* constructs a UPPAAL model from the given AST of the SystemC design. The model is incrementally build and stored in an *internal representation*. Second, the *optimization engine* performs several optimizations on that. Accordingly, the implementation of STATE consists of three packages: the package `model` contains classes for the internal representation of both the SystemC and the timed automata model. The package `engine` contains classes that implement the transformation rules from SystemC to UPPAAL. The package `optimization` contains several optimizations to make the generated UPPAAL model smaller and easier to read. In the following, we present content and structure of the three packages.

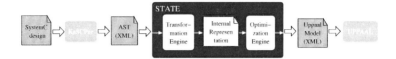

Figure 7.2: Tool chain from SystemC to Uppaal

Internal Representations

During the course of the transformation from SystemC to UPPAAL, a UP-PAAL model is incrementally build. When the SystemC design is read in, some elements, like methods, are directly transformed into corresponding UPPAAL templates. For other SystemC elements, like a module instantiation, the information must be saved for later design composition. To collect such information and to store the gradually growing UPPAAL model, we use the classes SCModel and TAModel. In SCModel, information about SystemC modules is stored, for example, their ports, variables, events, functions, processes, and their constructor. This is necessary for later design composition. Furthermore, the class SCModel contains a set of module instances. In TAModel, templates, template instances, and global declarations are stored. The templates consist of locations and transitions and hold references to variables that are used locally or as parameters. With SCModel and TAModel together, all relevant information for the transformation can be internally represented. When the transformation phase is finished, TAModel contains the complete UPPAAL model.

Transformation Engine

In the transformation engine, we use the Xerces DOM Parser [Apa06] to read the AST of the SystemC design. The idea is to define a dedicated handler function for each XML node. Those handler functions take as parameters an XML node, the current SCModel, the current TAModel and a hash map that collects other information like the current module or the current method. The concept of dedicated handler functions makes the implementation modular and flexible and eases further developments. Remember that we have two kinds of transformation rules. We have rules that directly map a SystemC language construct to a corresponding timed automata representation and rules that define templates for special SystemC constructs. Examples for the first type are the rules for method and statement transformation, examples for the latter are the rules for SystemC events, processes, and the request-update protocol. A special case of the latter type is the rule for the construction of the SystemC scheduler, which is added implicitly to every model to implement the scheduling semantics.

The transformation is performed in two phases: first, the SystemC model is read in and the information is stored in SCModel and TAModel. Functional parts of the SystemC design, i. e., methods, are directly translated into timed

automata templates. Structural information, which is necessary for instantiation and binding, is collected in `SCModel`. In the second phase, this information
is used to add global declarations and the system declaration to the `TAModel`.
With that, the `TAModel` can be completed. The result is then written to an
output XML file. However, not all parts of the generated `TAModel` are necessary to obtain a semantic-preserving UPPAAL model. In the following, we
describe several optimizations that remove such elements from the `TAModel`.

Optimization Engine

The aim of the optimization engine is to reduce the size of the generated UP-
PAAL model and to enhance its readability. The first is advantageous because
it reduces the computational effort of model checking and conformance test
generation. The second is advantageous because the UPPAAL model can be
used for debugging purposes. If a verification attempt fails, the UPPAAL model
checker provides a counter-example which can also be graphically visualized.
To make counter-examples as comprehensible as possible, the readability of
the generated UPPAAL model is very important.

During the course of the transformation of a given SystemC design, it is not
always possible to avoid the generation of superfluous elements. This is due to
the modular structure of the transformation engine, where each SystemC construct is separately handled, and thus not all semantic information is available
in each handler function. For example, for the transformation of a SystemC
event, an event template is used which provides an interface for notifying the
event immediately, delta-delayed, or with a timing delay. If the event is only
notified immediately, the other parameters from the interface are dispensable.
The optimization engine detects such unused elements and deletes them from
the `TAModel`. The following optimizations are implemented at the time:

- **Unused template parameters**
  This optimization checks for each parameter of a template whether it is
  actually used and deletes it otherwise. This improves readability of the
  generated model.

- **Unused template instantiations**
  Each method is instantiated once for each process that could use it. This
  optimizations checks for each method template instantiation whether it
  is actually used and deletes it otherwise. This improves readability and
  reduces the number of locations in the semantic state space.

- **Unused events**
  For each process, a dedicated timeout event is generated to realize timed
  wait-statements. This optimization detects event templates that are
  never used and deletes them. This improves readability and reduces
  the number of locations and clocks in the semantic state space.

- **Non-preemptive transition chains**
  As the transformation of each statement is done separately, a chain of

non-preemptive statements is transformed to a chain of transitions, where one action is assigned to each transition. Such non-preemptive chains are merged to a single transition associated with a sequence of actions. This improves the readability of the generated model.

With the presented optimizations, a given SystemC design can be automatically translated into a compact and easily comprehensible UPPAAL model. Furthermore, the modular approach of the separation between transformation and optimization together with the dedicated handler functions makes the implementation flexible and eases further developments.

7.2 ATENA

In Chapter 6, we presented an algorithm for the generation of conformance tests from a given UPPAAL timed automata model. The algorithm takes a network of timed automata as input and computes all possible output traces for a given input trace, which is in our case already contained in the UPPAAL model. The resulting set of output traces can then be used for automated conformance evaluation. We implemented the basic algorithm in the diploma thesis of Florian Friedemann [Fri09]. The result is the **A**utomated **T**est generation **E**ngine for **N**on-deterministic Timed **A**utomata (ATENA). We extended and optimized ATENA in the diploma thesis of Marcel Pockrandt [Poc09]. As ATENA computes all possible output traces of the given UPPAAL model, it must explore the whole state space that is reachable with the input trace contained in the model. To make the exploration of the state space as efficient as possible, ATENA generates an executable representation from the UPPAAL model. In the executable representation, semantically related elements are directly linked, and expressions are simplified whenever possible. The executable representation is executed by a *symbolic executor* that explores the state space and that constructs a partial computation tree, which contains all possible output traces.

Figure 7.3 shows the structure of ATENA. The input UPPAAL model is given in XML format. We used ANTLR (ANother Tool for Language Recognition) [Par08] for the automatic generation of a parser from the NTA *grammar*. The grammar defines a set of rules that describe the syntax of the input language and that map each language element to the output language. ANTLR also allows the automatic generation of translators and code generation. In ATENA, we defined two grammars: the *NTA grammar* describes the input *Network of Timed Automata* (NTA), and the *AST grammar* describes the *abstract syntax tree* (AST). For the construction of the *executable representation* (ER), we defined a set of *string templates* and a set of *translation rules*. The string templates describe the Java classes that constitute the ER. The translation rules describe how the AST is translated to the ER. We use ANTLR to generate a *parser* from the NTA grammar, and a *translator* from the AST grammar and the string templates together with the translation rules. For the generation of an executable representation, a given UPPAAL model is first

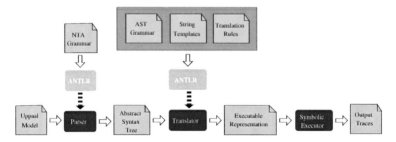

Figure 7.3: ATENA

parsed and then translated into an ER. Finally, the ER is used by the *Symbolic Executor* to compute all possible output traces.

Overall, the implementation of ATENA consists of two parts: first, the grammars together with the string templates and the translation rules used to generate the executable representation. Second, the symbolic executor together with several helper classes for the operations on Difference Bound Matrices (DBM) are used to explore the state space and to generate all possible output traces. In the following, we first present the main characteristics of the executable representation and then those of the symbolic executor.

Executable Representation

In the first phase of ATENA, an executable representation is generated from the input model. To this end, the class *ER* is constructed which contains an efficiently executable representation of the network of timed automata. The class *ER* is automatically generated by the chained application of the *parser* and of the *translator*. It mainly consists of the appropriate instantiations of predefined classes for processes, locations, edges, variables, clocks, and channels. Each process contains a set of locations, a set of edges, a reference to its initial location, and a reference to the global data space. With that, the network can be efficiently executed as follows: first, the current location is taken from each process. Then all possible successor states are computed (as described in Section 6.4). Finally each process is set to the corresponding next location.

Locations and edges can be associated with invariants, guards, and updates on global variables. To make the evaluation of guards and invariants and the execution of updates as efficient as possible, the expressions are simplified and transformed into executable methods. For example, each edge has a method *performAction()* that directly executes the sequence of actions assigned to the edge as *updates* in the UPPAAL model. Similarly, the method *getClockGuards()* directly evaluates the parts of the edge's guard that refer to global variables. It returns either *null* if this already leads to *false* or a list of clock guards.

The latter are conjuncted with the current DBM to check whether the guard is satisfiable in the current clock zone.

Symbolic Executor

The symbolic executor implements the test generation algorithm (Listing 6.1). It starts with the initial symbolic state of a given network of timed automata, computes all possible successor states and then all possible successor states for those and so on until the complete state space that is reachable with the given input trace is explored. The result is a partial computation tree, from which the possible set of output traces can be derived.

The heart of the test generation algorithm is the function `getSuccessors(s)` that computes all possible successor states of a given state. This function implements the complete symbolic semantics of UPPAAL as presented in Section 6.2. Symbolic states are triples $\langle \bar{l}, D, v \rangle$, where $\bar{l}$ is a vector of locations, D a difference bound matrix representing a clock zone, and v a vector of variable assignments. The class `State` is used to represent symbolic states. It contains a unique identifier, a list of locations, a DBM, and a list of variable values. In addition, the flags `endState` and `deadlock` are used to indicate whether the state denotes the end of the test case or a deadlock state, respectively. From a given state together with the executable representation generated from the input UPPAAL model, all possible successor states are computed. During the state space exploration, semantic states have to be kept in memory to detect cycles. This leads to a state space explosion and the test generation algorithm may run *out of memory*. To solve this problem, we presented several optimizations in Section 6.4.3. The proposed optimizations exploit the specifics of the SystemC semantics to drastically reduce the number of states that have to be kept in memory. To this end, they make use of delta-cycles, the cooperative scheduler, and linear time progression. All of these optimizations were also implemented in the symbolic executor.

With the presented optimizations, ATENA efficiently explores the state space of a given UPPAAL model and computes a partial computation tree. From that, all output traces that are possible with a given input trace can be derived. The generated set of output traces can be used to generate SystemC test benches for the automated conformance evaluation of a given SystemC design.

7.3 TBGeneSys

The Test Bench Generator for SystemC (TBGeneSys) parses the set of output traces yielded by ATENA, and generates a SystemC test bench from that as described in Section 6.5. The test bench is constructed from the manually implemented output monitor that was also used for conformance test generation (cf. Section 6.1). All ports and declarations are kept, but the monitor function is deleted and replaced by automatically generated monitor functions that compare the outputs of the system under test with the previously computed expected output traces. Furthermore, the constructor is replaced by one that declares the corresponding processes, and some global variable declarations (e. g., a state variable) are added. Apart from that, the generated test bench contains a look-up table (LUT) as described in Section 6.5. The LUT is used to check in each state whether the variable values are correct, whether a valid successor state is reached, and whether timing constraints are adhered to. If one of these conditions is not satisfied, the test verdict is *fail* and test execution is aborted. If an inconclusive state is reached, the test verdict is *inconclusive*. If a valid end state is reached, the test verdict is *pass*. Note that in the case of multiple output monitors in the original test bench, all of these monitors are replaced by monitors that automatically check the conformance of the outputs of the design under test with those computed from the abstract design.

8 Experimental Results

The implementation of the VeriSTA framework allows the practical evaluation of our approach. The most important measures for the practical applicability are the performance and the error detecting capability of the framework. We evaluated these measures with a set of experiments. The performance is measured in terms of computational effort. To illustrate the efficiency of our tool chain, we provide experimental results that show the computational effort of both the transformation with STATE and the test bench generation with ATENA and TBGeneSys. Furthermore, to demonstrate the applicability of the overall framework, we also provide experimental results that measure the computational effort of the verification of SystemC designs using the UPPAAL model checker. Those experiments show the compactness of the UPPAAL models generated with STATE. To evaluate the error detecting capability of our conformance testing approach, we generated test benches and executed them against erroneous designs. We obtain erroneous designs by injecting defects from a predefined set of fault classes.

In the following, we first briefly present the main characteristics of the three designs we use as case studies, namely a small producer-consumer example, the packet switch example from the SystemC reference implementation, and a SystemC design of an Anti-Slip Regulation and Anti-lock Braking System (ABS/ASR). Then, we present our results from the performance evaluation of our framework. Finally, we provide experimental results that demonstrate the error detecting capability of our conformance testing approach.

8.1 Case Studies

For our practical evaluation, we use three case studies: a producer-consumer example, a packet switch example and an ABS/ASR system. Note that the producer-consumer and the packet switch example are especially well-suited to assess performance and scalability of our approach because we can vary the size of the designs. The ABS is especially well-suited to assess the error-detecting capability of our conformance test approach because it was developed

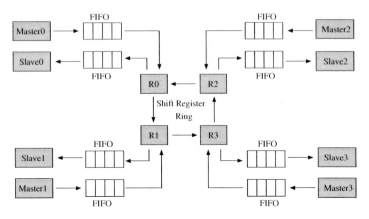

Figure 8.1: Architecture of the Packet Switch

in a typical refinement flow following the transaction level modeling (TLM) approach and we have an abstract design and a refined design available.

Producer-Consumer Example

The producer-consumer example was already used to illustrate the main language elements of SystemC in Section 2.4. It consists of a producer and a consumer that communicate through a *first in first out* (FIFO) buffer. It uses the SystemC channel concept as well as static, dynamic, and timing sensitivity and thus covers many important language constructs of SystemC. Note that the design is non-deterministic, as the execution order of producer and consumer is not pre-determined. For our experiments, we use the producer-consumer example with a varying buffer size. With that, we obtain a preliminary assessment of the scalability of our approach. The size of the producer-consumer example is approximately 130 lines of code (LOC) and it consists of two modules, two processes and one channel.

Packet Switch

The packet switch example is taken from the SystemC reference implementation and demonstrates a multi-cast packet switch. The switch uses a self routing ring of shift registers to transfer cells from one port to another in a pipelined fashion, resolving output contention and efficiently handling multicast cells. Input and output ports have FIFO buffers of depth 16 each.[1] The architecture of the packet switch is shown in Figure 8.1.

---

[1] This description is mainly taken from the README file of the SystemC reference implementation.

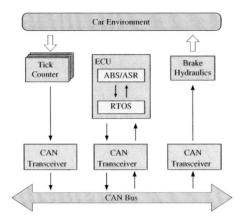

Figure 8.2: Architecture of the ABS/ASR System

For our experiments, we use the packet switch example with a varying number of masters and slaves, from one master and one slave up to four of each. With that, the packet switch example is especially well-suited for the evaluation of the scalability of our framework. The size of the packet switch example is approximately 400 LOC. It contains 5 modules, 5 processes and 6 channels in case of one master and one slave, and 5 modules, 11 processes and 15 channels in case of four masters and four slaves.

Anti-lock Braking System and Anti-Slip Regulation

The ABS/ASR system monitors the speed of each wheel and regulates the brake pressure in order to prevent wheel lockup or loss of traction and to improve the driver's control over the car. It consists of dedicated wheel speed sensors, a hydraulic modulator to control the brake pressure, an electronic control unit that runs the control algorithms, and a control area network (CAN) bus. The architecture of the design is shown in Figure 8.2. To measure the wheel speed, the number of incoming wheel signals (ticks) are used to compute the speed of each wheel. To this end, a *tick counter* is placed of each wheel. The measurement results are sent to an electronic control unit (ECU) via a CAN bus. On the ECU, the control algorithms for brake pressure control and Anti-Slip-Regulation (ASR) are executed. A minimal real-time operating system (RTOS) is used to schedule the tasks in the ECU and provides an interrupt layer for the interactions with the CAN bus. The resulting control signals are sent to the brake hydraulics.

The ABS was developed in a student's project using a typical HW/SW co-design flow following the TLM approach. We started with an abstract design where processes communicate over FIFO channels and where timing is only coarsely estimated. This abstract model allows the validation and verification of the control algorithm without having to cope with communication or timing details. Then, we refined the design by using a high-speed CAN bus for communication, an interrupt layer and simple scheduling algorithm on the electronic control unit, and detailed timing information. While the abstract design consists of approximately 500 LOC and contains 4 modules and 18 processes that communicate over 12 channels, the refined design consists of over 5 KLOC and contains 10 modules and 28 processes that communicate over 25 channels. Overall, the ABS is well-suited to assess the performance and error detecting capability of our approach. We can use the abstract design to generate conformance tests and then automatically evaluate conformance of the refined design.

8.2 Performance Evaluation

For the evaluation of the performance of our framework, we measured the computational effort of

- the transformation of a given SystemC design into a UPPAAL model,
- model checking of an automatically generated UPPAAL model,
- the generation of SystemC test benches for automated conformance evaluation from an automatically generated UPPAAL model for a given test scenario.

The results are presented in the following sections. All experiments were run on a machine with an Intel Pentium 3.4 GHz DualCore CPU and 4 GB main memory running a Linux operating system.

8.2.1 Transformation from SystemC to Uppaal

Table 8.1 shows the results for the computational effort of the transformation from SystemC to UPPAAL for the three case studies. The results show that the transformation time is negligible and that it scales well for an increasing number of modules. This is due to our modular transformation approach. The computational effort of the main translation phase is linear in the number of modules and the code size, and the computational effort of the design composition is linear in the number of module instances. In the parsing phase, the AST of the design as produced by KaSCPar is read in node by node. Thus, the parse time is linear in the code size. The optimizations remove unused elements, i.e., they process the design only once. Thus, the optimization time is also linear in the code size.

	Transformation Time (in seconds)				
	Parse	Translate	Compose	Optimize	Total
Producer-Consumer	0.08	0.18	0.00	0.07	0.33
Packet Switch 1m1s	0.28	0.31	0.01	0.22	0.82
Packet Switch 1m2s	0.32	0.33	0.02	0.24	0.91
Packet Switch 2m1s	0.32	0.31	0.02	0.27	0.92
Packet Switch 2m2s	0.42	0.33	0.02	0.26	1.02
Packet Switch 4m4s	0.79	0.38	0.04	0.29	1.50
ABS/ASR System	0.45	0.36	0.03	0.24	1.08

Table 8.1: Computational Effort of the Transformation from SystemC to UPPAAL

8.2.2 Model Checking

For the evaluation of the performance of model checking of an automatically generated UPPAAL model, we verified liveness and safety properties using the UPPAAL model checker on all three case studies. To ensure the correctness of the designs for all possible input scenarios, we used generic input generation components. These components provide all possible inputs at arbitrary times. As a consequence, we obtain guarantees for all possible input scenarios.

Producer-Consumer Example

For the producer-consumer example, we verified the following properties:

(1) deadlock freedom,

(2) the absence of buffer overflows,

(3) the consumer reads items sent by the producer within a given time limit.

	Verification Time (in seconds)				
Property	BS 10	BS 50	BS 100	BS 1000	satisfied
(1)	1.78	1.78	1.78	1.81	✓
(2)	1.78	1.78	1.78	1.81	✓
(3)	1.82	1.95	9.22	10851	✓

Table 8.2: Results from Model Checking of the Producer-Consumer Example for Varying Buffer Sizes (BS)

We varied the buffer size of the FIFO connecting the producer and the consumer from 10 to 1000 (BS 10, BS 50, BS 100, BS 1000). In all cases, all properties were proved correct. Table 8.2 shows the verification times averaged over 10 runs. Note that the first two properties can be expressed by simple CTL formulae, while the third property is not directly expressible in CTL. This is due to the fact that we need to track each item until it arrives at the consumer. To this end, we introduced an additional helper automaton, which copies the values the producer sends into an internal array and deletes them when they are read by the consumer within the given time limit. If they are not read within the given time limit, it reaches a failure location. The CTL formula for the third property is then simply that the helper automaton never reaches this failure location. As shown in Table 8.2, the verification effort for the first two properties is small and scales comparatively well. For the third property, it is much higher and less scalable. This is due to the large internal array that is used in the helper automaton.

Packet Switch Example

For the verification of the packet switch example, we checked the following properties:

(1) deadlock freedom,

(2) every packet is forwarded to all its receivers, and

(3) if a packet is forwarded, this is done within a given time limit.

For the third property, we used a similar helper automaton as for the producer-consumer example. In this case, however, the amount of data that has to be stored internally in the helper automaton is limited due to the limited space in the packet switch shift ring. In all experiments, we increased the number of masters and slaves from one master and one slave up to two master and two slaves (1m1s, 1m2s, 2m1s, 2m2s). Table 8.3 presents the verification times averaged over 10 runs. In all cases, properties (1.) and (3.) were found satisfied, while property (2.) is not satisfied. The reason for that is as follows: Due to the semantics of sc_signal, the change event of signal ports is only notified if the value changes. If consecutively sent messages are equal, there is no change event at the input port of the packet switch and thus, only the first message is forwarded. This is a typical corner case which is both hard to find and hard to trace and understand with standard simulation. With our approach, we found it automatically and instantly had a graphically animated counter-example at hand to easily find out where the problem arose from. Note that the generation of counter-examples is very fast, as it is not necessary to explore the complete state-space. This makes debugging fast and efficient. The results show that verification of properties (1.) and (3.) scales comparatively well for this case study.

Property	Verification Time (in seconds)				satisfied
	1m1s	2m1s	1m2s	2m2s	
(1)	22.28	56.49	43.73	211.26	✓
(2)	3.02	3.38	3.30	4.89	↯
(3)	129.16	46.63	298.41	544.88	✓

Table 8.3: Results from Model Checking of the Packet Switch for Varying Numbers of Masters (m) and Slaves (s)

ABS and ASR System

For the ABS/ASR example, the generic input generation component sends ticks for each wheel in arbitrary time intervals, but with a minimal distance corresponding to 200 km/h. The maximal distance between two ticks is unlimited, as the car may also stop for an arbitrary amount of time. Overall, the component allows arbitrary speeds up to the maximal speed of 200 km/h and also enables arbitrary acceleration and deceleration. We checked the following properties on the abstract ABS/ASR design:

(1) deadlock freedom,

(2) if the deceleration exceeds a given limit, i. e., the wheels lock, the brake pressure is eventually reduced,

(3) if the deceleration exceeds a given limit, the brake pressure is reduced within a given time limit,

(4) if the acceleration exceeds a given limit, i. e., the wheels slip, the brake pressure is eventually increased,

(5) if the acceleration exceeds a given limit, the brake pressure is increased within a given time limit.

In the beginning, only the first property turned out to be satisfied. With little debugging effort, supported by the counter-examples produced by the model checker, we found out where the problem arose from. We made an error during the conversion of ticks into speed. This error was not detected by our previously used test cases because we unintentionally solely used test cases where changes in the tick speed happened only at full seconds. Note again that the generation of counter-examples is very fast. After the defect removal, the state space turned out to be too large to be completely explored with our 4 GB main memory. This is mainly due to the large data ranges used in the ABS/ASR example, which cannot symbolically be captured by the UPPAAL model checker. However, with bit state hashing enabled, we were able to verify that the properties are *maybe* satisfied. The result of model checking with bit state hashing is an under-approximation of the state space, i. e., the state space is only partially explored. However, it is still very well-suited for debugging purposes. Furthermore, given that a large hash table is available, it can be

	Computation Time (in seconds)			
	Generation of		Property	
Property	Counter-Examples		Verification	
(1)	-	-	722.54	✓ (maybe)
(2)	2.56	⚡	555.56	✓ (maybe)
(3)	3.51	⚡	844.15	✓ (maybe)
(4)	2.13	⚡	556.78	✓ (maybe)
(5)	2.95	⚡	532.93	✓ (maybe)

Table 8.4: Results from Model Checking of the ABS/ASR System

expected that the verification results have a high probability to be reliable if the model checker does not find a counter-example.

8.2.3 Conformance Test Generation

To evaluate our conformance testing approach, we computed all possible output traces for our three case studies. As a test scenario for the producer-consumer example, we used a trace where hundred items are sent from the producer to the consumer. In case of the packet switch, we used consecutively sent packages with fixed data until each receiver has received at least two packages. As a test scenario for the ABS/ASR system, we simulated an acceleration from 0 km/h to 200 km/h at full throttle and a subsequent deceleration with full application of the brakes. Our test scenario ensures that both the ASR and the ABS come into action and run through the whole control cycles.

For the three case studies, we performed conformance test generation using the basic algorithm as well as the optimized version. We already used the packet switch example with up to two masters and two slaves in [HFG09] and we use it now to illustrate the effect of the optimizations of the conformance test algorithm. The resulting computation time and memory usage averaged over 10 runs are shown in Table 8.5. Only for the producer-consumer example, the optimizations do not pay off and the optimized version is slightly slower than the basic version. For the packet switch, the computation time is reduced by 50 - 60%, the memory usage by over 90%. The packet switch example with four masters and four slaves and the ABS/ASR system ran out of memory with the basic algorithm, but can be handled in reasonable time with the optimized version.

	CPU Time (s)			Memory Usage (MB)		
	Base	Optim	Improv	Base	Optim	Improv
Producer-Consumer	4.90	5.07	-3.5%	5	5	0%
Packet Switch 1m1s	25.11	9.49	62.2%	58	5	91.4%
Packet Switch 1m2s	34.27	13.90	59.4%	98	5	94.9%
Packet Switch 2m1s	42.38	20.72	51.1%	160	5	96.9%
Packet Switch 2m2s	54.77	27.43	49.9%	275	13	95.3%
Packet Switch 4m4s	↯	443	∞	↯	302	∞
ABS/ASR System	↯	10210	∞	↯	302	∞

Table 8.5: Computational Effort of Conformance Test Generation

8.3 Error Detecting Capability

To evaluate the error detecting capability of our conformance testing approach, we used the same test scenarios as described above. We generated SystemC test benches for automated conformance evaluation as described in Section 6.5. Then, we injected several defects from the following fault classes into the designs:

- missing and wrong condition
- missing and wrong assignment
- permuted variables
- transmission error
- transmission delay

In case of the producer-consumer and the packet switch example, we injected defects into the designs themselves. Then, we generated SystemC test benches from the original designs and executed them against the faulty versions. In case of the ABS/ASR system, we have an abstract and a refined design available. We injected defects into the refined design according to the predefined set of fault classes. Table 8.6 shows the results. Then, we generated test benches from the abstract model and executed them against the refined design.

For the producer-consumer example, we have ambiguous results. Some defects are detected, others are not detected. This is due to the non-deterministic behavior of the example and the incomplete statement coverage of the test scenario. For example, the FIFO buffer is never completely filled in the given test scenario. As a consequence, a manipulation of the condition that prevents a buffer overflow does not lead to a failure. Similarly, a wrong assignment is not always detected. For example, it is not detected if it only affects the

	Producer-Consumer	Packet Switch	ABS/ASR System
without defects	*pass*	*pass*	*pass*
missing or wrong condition	*pass*/*fail*	*fail*	*fail*
missing or wrong assignment	*pass*/*fail*	*fail*	*fail*
permuted variables	*fail*	*fail*	*fail*
transmission delay or loss	*fail*	*fail*	*fail*

Table 8.6: Error Detecting Capability

variable counting the number of items currently stored in the FIFO buffer and the FIFO buffer becomes neither full nor empty. However, these are standard problems in the area of black-box testing. Standard solutions are the use of test suites with full coverage and the repeated execution of test cases in case of non-deterministic behavior.

For the packet switch and the ABS/ASR system, all defects were detected, i. e., each deviation from the specification was detected. This has two reasons: first, the full statement coverage of our test scenario, and second, that all injected defects led to an observable deviation from the specification. With a test scenario that does not cover all parts of the control cycles, we would not be able to detect all kinds of defects. However, as we assume the test scenario (or input trace) as given, we are not interested in the coverage of a certain test suite so far. The important result here is that we can detect all kinds of defects with our automated conformance evaluation, given that the considered test scenario reveals the erroneous behavior. The fact that for both case studies each of the injected defects had impact on the observed output behavior is a specialty of the case studies. In general, errors that do not lead to a deviation from the specification in the output traces are never detectable with black-box testing approaches. However, they are strictly speaking not considered as a defect in our sense.

8.4 Summary

Overall, our experiments demonstrate the applicability, the performance, and the error detecting capability of our approach. The computational effort of the transformation from SystemC to UPPAAL is linear in the number of modules and in the code size. It takes only a few seconds even for comparably large designs. Concerning the model checking of SystemC designs, we encountered the problem of state space explosion. However, we have shown that it is possible to obtain *guarantees* about the liveness and timing behavior for our smaller case studies. It covers corner cases that are hard to find with testing and simulation. For example, we detected a problem in the SystemC reference implementation of the packet switch example that results in a failure only for very special test scenarios. As the UPPAAL model checker generates counter-examples if a proof attempt fails, the source of a failure is easily detectable. This is in particular supported by the graphical visualization of counter-examples. For larger case studies, such as the ABS/ASR system, we were not able to *guarantee* liveness and timing properties because the model checker ran out of memory. However, the model checking approach is still very useful for these systems, as it can be used for debugging purposes. The generation of counter-examples is very fast and efficient even for large systems. We detected a defect in the ABS/ASR system that we had not detected with testing. Furthermore, the possibility of bit state hashing available in the UPPAAL model checker allows a partial exploration of the state space that fully exploits the available memory. This does not yield guarantees about the behavior of a SystemC design, but the probability that errors are not detected is very low if the model checker could not find a counter-example with a large hash table. However, the efficiency of model checking itself is out of the scope of this thesis. The aim of our work is to provide a formal semantics for SystemC, and to make model checking and conformance testing applicable to SystemC designs. Our experimental results show that we have met that goal.

The experimental results of our conformance testing approach are very promising. Conformance tests can be generated even for large systems, as the reachable state space is limited by the length of the input trace. The computational effort of the conformance test generation is notable, but acceptable as it only has to be done once, and then the test cases can be repeated arbitrarily often without re-computation. The experiments on the error detecting capability show that all kinds of errors can in principle be detected with our approach. The actual amount of detected errors depends on the coverage of the given test suite.

9 Conclusion

In this chapter, we summarize and discuss the results of this thesis. We also review the criteria we defined in the introduction and discuss whether we succeeded in meeting them. Then, we give an outlook on future work.

9.1 Results

In this thesis, we presented our approach for the automated HW/SW co-verification of SystemC designs using timed automata. The approach allows the fully automatic verification of digital HW/SW systems modeled in SystemC. It is based on a quality assurance process that assists the HW/SW co-design flow efficiently and continuously from an abstract design down to the final implementation. The general idea is to formally verify abstract designs via model checking and to generate conformance tests for all subsequent refinements of the abstract design. This combination is especially well-suited for HW/SW co-verification, as it can be applied to both the hardware and the software parts of a given HW/SW co-design on different levels of abstraction. Furthermore, both the model checking and the conformance testing are automatically applicable.

We presented a concept for a comprehensive and formally well-founded quality assurance process. Our framework for the automated **Veri**fication of **S**ystemC designs using **T**imed **A**utomata (VeriSTA) puts the proposed process into practice and allows automated verification of SystemC designs throughout the whole design flow. The prerequisite for the application of automated verification techniques is a formal semantics of SystemC. We solved this problem by defining a transformation from SystemC to UPPAAL timed automata. The resulting UPPAAL model can be used as input for the UPPAAL model checker, and thus we can prove that it meets a given requirements specification fully automatically. Furthermore, it yields a formal basis for automated conformance test generation.

Our approach for model checking SystemC designs is based on a mapping from the informally defined semantics of SystemC to the formally well-defined semantics of UPPAAL timed automata. Based on this mapping, a SystemC design can be transformed into a semantically equivalent UPPAAL model. Furthermore, the formal model of a given design can be derived automatically. That means that the designer does not have to perform the time-consuming and error-prone task of developing a formal model any more. The transformation enables the usage of the UPPAAL tool suite on SystemC designs. This includes the UPPAAL model checker to formally verify temporal properties of SystemC designs, and the animated simulation of counter-examples for debugging purposes. For the transformation, SystemC processes are transformed into timed automata processes, which are synchronized using channels. The execution semantics is modeled using an explicit model of the scheduler together with specific templates for events and processes. The translation is performed fully automatically. We use a compositional approach where modules are translated separately. Thus, the approach is highly scalable, and complex and large SystemC designs can be transformed in reasonable time. The informally defined behavior of a given SystemC design is completely preserved in the generated UPPAAL model. In addition to that, also the structure of the design is preserved. This makes it easy for the designer to locate possible errors in the SystemC design based on the counter-example the model checker provides if the verification fails. Moreover, the models generated by our method are compact and easily comprehensible and can comparatively efficiently be verified by model checking. This is demonstrated by our experimental results.

In addition to the transformation from SystemC to UPPAAL, we presented an approach for the automated conformance evaluation of SystemC designs. To this end, we presented a complete symbolic semantics for UPPAAL timed automata. Furthermore, we defined a formal conformance relation that can be used to relate an implementation in SystemC to a specification in UPPAAL. Based on the symbolic UPPAAL semantics and on the conformance relation, we presented an algorithm for the generation of conformance tests from a given UPPAAL timed automata model. The algorithm can cope with *non-deterministic* designs and computes all possible expected output traces for a given input trace *offline*. To the best of our knowledge, such an approach was never investigated before. To mitigate the effect of the state space explosion problem, we presented several optimizations that make use of the specifics of the SystemC semantics to drastically reduce the number of semantic states that have to be kept in memory during state space exploration. Furthermore, we presented an approach to automatically generate SystemC test benches that allow fully automatic conformance evaluation.

For the practical evaluation of our approach, we implemented the complete VeriSTA framework. The implementation consists of three components: The SystemC to Timed Automata Transformation Engine (STATE) translates a given SystemC design into a semantically equivalent UPPAAL model. The Automated Test generation Engine for Non-deterministic Timed Automata (ATENA) computes all possible output traces from a given UPPAAL model. The Test Bench Generator for SystemC (TBGeneSys) generates SystemC test benches that allow fully automatic conformance evaluation. To evaluate the applicability of our approach, we used three case studies: a simple producer-consumer example, the packet switch example from the SystemC reference implementation, and an Anti-Slip Regulation and Anti-lock Braking System (ABS/ASR) developed in a student's project. The experimental results show the automated applicability and the error detecting capability of our approach. The generated UPPAAL models can be comparatively efficiently verified using the UPPAAL model checker, and conformance tests are generated in reasonable time. In particular, the presented optimizations of the algorithm for conformance test generation succeeded in reducing the computational effort and the memory consumption significantly. Finally, the experiments demonstrate that the generated SystemC test benches can be used for fully automatic conformance evaluation and that defects can efficiently be detected.

9.2 Discussion

In the introducing chapter, we defined a set of criteria that a framework for the automated HW/SW co-verification of SystemC designs should meet. In addition, we also defined a set of criteria for a formal semantics of SystemC. In the following, we first review and discuss the criteria we defined for the overall framework, and then those for the formal semantics of SystemC.

First, we stated that the proposed co-verification techniques must be suitable for both hardware and software parts of a given digital control system, and that they have to be able to cope with the main co-design concepts, namely concurrency, time, reactivity, hierarchical modeling and abstract communication. Due to the implementation of concurrency in the SystemC scheduler, this includes the requirement to support non-deterministic system designs. Our framework VeriSTA meets all these requirements. It is suitable for both hardware and software and for the main co-design concepts, as it supports all relevant SystemC language constructs. This includes delta-cycles and the request-update scheme, static and dynamic sensitivity, timing behavior, and the communication model of SystemC. Furthermore, the non-deterministic behavior of the SystemC scheduler is explicitly modeled. This allows the verification of all possible execution orders in case of concurrent execution.

Second, we claimed that the quality assurance process should be comprehensive and *continuous*, in other words, it should support the complete system design flow from an abstract design down to the final implementation. This requirement is met by the combination of model checking and conformance testing. As model checking is applied on an abstract design and conformance tests are generated for each refined design, the design flow is continuously supported. The conformance testing also ensures consistency between different abstraction levels in a refinement process and allows the reuse of verification results from high abstraction levels on lower abstraction levels.

Third, we required the co-verification techniques proposed in our quality assurance process to be automatically applicable and efficient. In our VeriSTA framework, the only manual effort that is necessary is the specification of the requirements in temporal logics. Everything else can be done automatically, as our experimental results demonstrate. In the current development state, the test inputs have to be defined manually. We are already working on an extension of our framework with the possibility of automatic input selection. The efficiency of our framework, in particular the efficiency of model checking, is limited by the state space explosion problem. However, this inherent problem of model checking is beyond the scope of this thesis. Still, the UPPAAL models we generate are compact and thus, our approach is *comparatively efficient*.

In addition to the criteria we defined for an overall HW/SW co-verification framework, we also defined a set of criteria for a formal semantics of SystemC. We required the formal semantics to preserve the behavioral semantics and the structure of a given SystemC design. This is ensured by our semantic-preserving transformation that also preserves the structure of a given design. In addition, we claimed that a formal model should be generated automatically for a given design, that the generated model should be suitable for automated verification, and that there should be tool support to edit, visualize and simulate the formal model of a given SystemC design. Those criteria are all met by our approach to generate a UPPAAL model from a given SystemC design. With that, we obtain access to the complete UPPAAL tool suite, which allows the verification, visualization, and simulation of timed automata models.

9.3 Outlook

We presented a comprehensive and formally founded framework for the automated HW/SW co-verification of SystemC designs using timed automata. The framework supports the co-design of digital HW/SW systems throughout the whole development process and can be applied fully automatically. Furthermore, we implemented the complete framework and could show its practical applicability with our experimental results. In particular, we demonstrated the performance and the error detecting capability of our approach. However, there are still open questions that are worth to be investigated in further research.

For example, we are currently extending our framework with the ability to select input traces based on dedicated SystemC coverage criteria. Dedicated coverage criteria are for example *channel coverage, communication coverage*, or *port coverage*. We plan to use those criteria together with classical coverage criteria such as *statement coverage, branch coverage*, and *path coverage*. We are confident that we can systematically test certain refinement steps with that. For example, when the communication architecture is refined following the TLM approach, the dedicated criteria shown above are very promising to purposefully test the correctness of these refinements. In particular, we plan to combine intra-module or intra-process coverage criteria with inter-module or communication coverage criteria. With that, we hope to achieve an optimal trade-off between the size of a test suite and its error detecting capability. With the ability to select input traces, we obtain a fully automatic co-verification framework that supports the whole SystemC design flow without any user-interaction except for the requirement specification.

The main advantage of our approach lies in its expressiveness and comprehensiveness. It has to be said that this comes at a price. While our approach can cope with highly heterogeneous systems, in particular with both hardware and software, itis not optimal for purely synchronous hardware models. Such models could be verified more efficiently with specialized approaches than with our universally applicable framework. This effect is mitigated partly by our combination of static and dynamic techniques, but there is still room for improvement. In particular, we think that many of the approaches discussed in the related works section could complement our framework and that new promising research topics could arise from a combination of the central concepts. For example, all of the approaches that can be used for the verification of SystemC designs on register transfer level [GD05, GKD05, GKD06] can be used together with our framework. While our framework is particularly useful to verify the high-level structure and the interactions between hardware and software, dedicated hardware verification techniques such as SAT solving are more efficient for the verification of low-level RTL components. Furthermore, the expressiveness of our approach pays off whenever abstract high-level models are available, but it has its limitations if pure hardware blocks (IP cores) should be included in a design from the beginning. It would be interesting to combine the work of Kroening [KS05, BKS08] and Große [GKD06] with our framework. For example, the automatic HW/SW partitioning proposed by Kroening et al. [KS05] could be applied first. Then, we could apply dedicated hardware verification techniques to synchronous hardware blocks and our framework to the verification of software parts and the overall communication architecture.

The combination of our framework with dedicated hardware verification techniques is also very promising to transfer it to other application domains, for example, to the verification of multiprocessor systems. A prerequisite for this is again a formal model. However, multiprocessor systems usually consist of highly heterogeneous components, which could for example be written in a hardware description language such as Verilog or VHDL, but also in a software language such as C or Java. There exist many approaches to build a formal model for each of those components, but those models are very different for the hardware and the software parts. To solve this problem, it is necessary to develop a formally well-defined interface between the hardware and the software blocks. One possible solution to establish such an interface between is to use abstraction techniques together with composition. The idea of that would be to build an abstraction of a given software component that can be used in hardware verification or the other way around. Another possible solution is to establish an interface between the corresponding verification tools. When the whole system is verified, a model checker could for example consult a SAT solver to determine the behavior of a hardware component.

As a short-term goal, the extension of our VeriSTA framework with automated input selection is promising to complete its comprehensiveness and its ability for fully automatic co-verification of digital HW/SW systems. For the long-term, we are convinced that the integrated, automated, and formally well-founded verification of digital hardware and software can be successfully applied to large and heterogeneous systems, for example, to multiprocessor systems. In particular, the integrated analysis of hardware and software allows the verification of the interplay between hardware and software, which is still difficult and often excluded in current quality assurance processes.

List of Figures

List of Listings

List of Tables

Bibliography

[Acc03]   Accellera. System Verilog 3.1 Accellera's Extensions to Verilog. www.systemverilog.org, 2003.

[AD94]   Rajeev Alur and David L. Dill. A Theory of Timed Automata. *Theoretical Computer Science*, 126:183–235, 1994.

[AHH93]   Rajeev Alur, Thomas A. Henzinger, and Pei-Hsin Ho. Automatic Symbolic Verification of Embedded Systems. pages 2–11, 1993.

[Apa06]   Apache Software Foundation. *The Apache Xerces Project – Xerces XML-Parser*, 2006. http://xerces.apache.org.

[BCG+97]   Felice Balarin, Massimiliano Chiodo, Paolo Giusto, Harry Hsieh, Attila Jurecska, Luciano Lavagno, Claudio Passerone, Alberto Sangiovanni-Vincentelli, Ellen Sentovich, Kei Suzuki, and Bassam Tabbara. *Hardware-software co-design of embedded systems: the POLIS approach*. Kluwer Academic Publishers, Norwell, MA, USA, 1997.

[BD05]   David C. Black and Jack Donovan. *SystemC: From the Ground Up*. Springer-Verlag New York, Inc., Secaucus, NJ, USA, 2005.

[BDL04]   Gerd Behrmann, Alexandre David, and Kim G. Larsen. A Tutorial on UPPAAL. In *Formal Methods for the Design of Real-Time Systems*, LNCS 3185, pages 200–236. Springer, 2004.

[Bel03]   Richard Bellman. *Dynamic Programming*. Dover Publications, 2003.

[Ber91]   Gilles Bernot. Testing Against Formal Specifications: A Theoretical View. In *Proceedings of the international joint conference on theory and practice of software development on Advances in distributed computing (ADC) and colloquium on com-*

*bining paradigms for software development (CCPSD) (TAPSOFT,
Vol.2)*, pages 99–119, 1991.

[BFS05]   Francesco Bruschi, Fabrizio Ferrandi, and Donatella Sciuto. A
          framework for the functional verification of SystemC models.
          International Journal on Parallel Programming, 33(6):667–695,
          2005.

[BK08]   Nicolas Blanc and Daniel Kroening. Race analysis for SystemC
          using Model Checking. In *IEEE/ACM International Conference
          on Computer-Aided Design (ICCAD)*, pages 356–363, Piscataway,
          NJ, USA, 2008. IEEE Press.

[BKS08]   Nicolas Blanc, Daniel Kroening, and Natasha Sharygina. Scoot:
          A Tool for the Analysis of SystemC Models. In *International
          Conference on Tools and Algorithms for Construction and Anal-
          ysis of Systems (TACAS)*, volume 4963 of *LNCS*, pages 467–470.
          Springer, 2008.

[BLL⁺95] Johan Bengtsson, Kim G. Larsen, Fredrik Larsson, Paul Petters-
          son, and Wang Yi. UPPAAL — a Tool Suite for Automatic Veri-
          fication of Real–Time Systems. In *Workshop on Verification and
          Control of Hybrid Systems*, LNCS 1066, pages 232–243. Springer,
          October 1995.

[Bro05]   Manfred Broy. Automotive software and systems engineering. In
          *Proceedings of the 2nd ACM/IEEE International Conference on
          Formal Methods and Models for Co-Design (MEMOCODE)*, pages
          143–149, Washington, DC, USA, 2005. IEEE Computer Society.

[BY04]   Johan Bengtsson and Wang Yi. Timed automata: Semantics,
          algorithms and tools. In *Lecture Notes on Concurrency and Petri
          Nets*, LNCS 3098, pages 87–124. Springer, 2004.

[CG03]   Lukai Cai and Daniel Gajski. Transaction level modeling: an
          overview. In *International Conference on Hardware/Software
          Codesign and System Synthesis (CODES+ISSS)*, pages 19–24.
          ACM press, 2003.

[CGP99]   Edmund Clarke, Orna Grumberg, and Doron Peled. *Model Check-
          ing*. MIT Press, 1999.

[CKSY05] Edmund Clarke, Daniel Kroening, Natasha Sharygina, and Karen
          Yorav. SATABS: SAT-based predicate abstraction for ANSI-C.
          In *Tools and Algorithms for the Construction and Analysis of*

Systems (TACAS 2005), volume 3440 of *LNCS*, pages 570–574. Springer Verlag, 2005.

[CO00] Rachel Cardell-Oliver. Conformance tests for real-time systems with timed automata specifications. *Formal Aspects of Computing*, 12(5):350–371, 2000.

[DG02] Rolf Drechsler and Daniel Große. Reachability Analysis for Formal Verification of SystemC. In *Euromicro Conference on Digital Systems Design (DSD)*, pages 337–340, 2002.

[DHD72] Ole-Johan Dahl, C. A. R. Hoare, and Edsger W. Dijkstra. *Structured programming*. Academic Press, London, New York, 1972.

[dSMAP04] Karina R. G. da Silva, Elmar U. K. Melcher, Guido Araujo, and Valdiney Alves Pimenta. An automatic testbench generation tool for a SystemC functional verification methodology. In *SBCCI '04: Proceedings of the 17th symposium on Integrated circuits and system design*, pages 66–70, New York, NY, USA, 2004. ACM Press.

[dVT00] Rene G. de Vries and Jan Tretmans. On-the-fly conformance testing using SPIN. *Software Tools for Technology Transfer*, 2(4):382–393, 2000.

[EHB93] Rolf Ernst, Jörg Henkel, and Thomas Benner. Hardware/Software Cosynthesis for Microcontrollers. *IEEE Design & Test of Computers*, pages 64–75, 1993.

[EN03] Roy Emek and Yehuda Naveh. Scheduling of transactions for system-level test-case generation. In *HLDVT '03: Proceedings of the Eighth IEEE International Workshop on High-Level Design Validation and Test Workshop*, page 149, Washington, DC, USA, 2003. IEEE Computer Society.

[Flo62] Robert W. Floyd. Algorithm 97: Shortest path. *Communications of the ACM*, 5(6):345, 1962.

[FZI] FZI Research Center for Information Technology. KaSCPar - Karlsruhe SystemC Parser Suite.

[GD04] Daniel Große and Rolf Drechsler. Checkers for SystemC designs. In *Formal Methods and Models for Codesign*, pages 171–178. IEEE Computer Society, 2004.

[GD05] Daniel Große and Rolf Drechsler. CheckSyC: an efficient property checker for RTL SystemC designs. In *IEEE International Symposium on Circuits and Systems (ISCAS)*, pages 4167–4170, 2005.

[Ghe05]   Frank Ghenassia. *Transaction Level Modeling with SystemC: TLM Concepts and Applications for Embedded Systems*. Springer US, 2005.

[GKD05]   Daniel Große, Ulrich Kühne, and Rolf Drechsler. HW/SW Co-Verification of a RISC CPU using Bounded Model Checking. In *IEEE International Workshop on Microprocessor Test and Verification (MTV)*, pages 133–137, 2005.

[GKD06]   Daniel Große, Ulrich Kühne, and Rolf Drechsler. HW/SW Co-Verification of Embedded Systems using Bounded Model Checking. In *Great Lakes Symposium on VLSI*, pages 43–48. ACM Press, 2006.

[GM93]   Rajesh Gupta and Giovanni De Micheli. Hardware/Software Cosynthesis for Digital Systems. *IEEE Design & Test of Computers*, pages 29–41, 1993.

[GPKD08]   Daniel Große, Hernan Peraza, Wolfgang Klingauf, and Rolf Drechsler. *Embedded Systems Specification and Design Languages*, chapter Measuring the Quality of a SystemC Testbench by Using Code Coverage Techniques, pages 73–86. Springer Netherlands, 2008.

[Gro02]   Thorsten Groetker. *System Design with SystemC*. Kluwer Academic Publishers, 2002.

[Har05]   Ian G. Harris. Hardware/software covalidation. *Computers and Digital Techniques*, 152(3):380–392, 2005.

[Her10]   Paula Herber. Automated HW/SW Co-Verification of SystemC Designs using Timed Automata. In *EDAA / ACM PhDForum at Design, Automation and Test in Europe (DATE)*, 2010.

[HFG08]   Paula Herber, Joachim Fellmuth, and Sabine Glesner. Model Checking SystemC Designs Using Timed Automata. In *International Conference on Hardware/Software Codesign and System Synthesis (CODES+ISSS)*, pages 131–136. ACM press, 2008.

[HFG09]   Paula Herber, Florian Friedemann, and Sabine Glesner. Combining Model Checking and Testing in a Continuous HW/SW Co-Verification Process. In *Tests and Proofs*, volume 5668 of *LNCS*.

Springer, 2009.

[HLM+08] Anders Hessel, Kim G. Larsen, Marius Mikucionis, Brian Nielsen, Paul Pettersson, and Arne Skou. *Formal Methods and Testing*, chapter Testing Real-Time Systems Using UPPAAL, pages 77 – 117. Springer, 2008.

[HLN+03] Anders Hessel, Kim G. Larsen, Brian Nielsen, Paul Petterson, and Arne Skou. Time-optimal test cases for real-time systems. In *Proceedings of the 3rd International Workshop on Formal Approaches to Testing of Software (FATES)*, LNCS 2931, pages 114–130. Springer, 2003.

[HMT06] Ali Habibi, Haja Moinudeen, and Sofiene Tahar. Generating Finite State Machines from SystemC. In *Design, Automation and Test in Europe (DATE)*, pages 76–81. IEEE Press, 2006.

[HNSY94] Thomas A. Henzinger, Xavier Nicollin, Joseph Sifakis, and Sergio Yovine. Symbolic model checking for real-time systems. *Inf. Comput.*, 111(2):193–244, 1994.

[HT05] Ali Habibi and Sofiène Tahar. An Approach for the Verification of SystemC Designs Using AsmL. In *Automated Technology for Verification and Analysis (ATVA)*, LNCS 3707, pages 69–83. Springer, 2005.

[IEE04] IEEE Standards Association. IEEE Standard 1012–2004 for Software Verification and Validation, 2004.

[IEE05] IEEE Standards Association. IEEE Std. 1666–2005, Open SystemC Language Reference Manual, 2005.

[JCdS07] Alair Dias Junior and Diogenes Junior Cecilio da Silva. Code-coverage Based Test Vector Generation for SystemC Designs. In *ISVLSI '07: Proceedings of the IEEE Computer Society Annual Symposium on VLSI*, pages 198–206, Washington, DC, USA, 2007. IEEE Computer Society.

[KC04] Daniel Kroening and Edmund Clarke. Checking Consistency of C and Verilog using Predicate Abstraction and Induction. In *Proceedings of the IEEE/ACM International Conference on Computer-Aided Design (ICCAD)*, pages 66–72. IEEE, November 2004.

[KCY03] Daniel Kroening, Edmund Clarke, and Karen Yorav. Behavioral

Consistency of C and Verilog Programs Using Bounded Model Checking. In *Proceedings of the Design Automation Conference (DAC)*, pages 368–371. ACM Press, 2003.

[KEP06] Daniel Karlsson, Petru Eles, and Zebo Peng. Formal verification of SystemC Designs using a Petri-Net based Representation. In *Design, Automation and Test in Europe (DATE)*, pages 1228–1233. IEEE Press, 2006.

[KL93] Asawaree Kalavade and Edward A. Lee. A Hardware/Software Codesign Methodology for DSP Applications. *IEEE Design & Test of Computers*, pages 16–28, 1993.

[Kli05] Wolfgang Klingauf. Systematic Transaction Level Modeling of Embedded Systems with SystemC. In *Design, Automation and Test in Europe (DATE)*, pages 566–567, 2005.

[KS05] Daniel Kroening and Natasha Sharygina. Formal Verification of SystemC by Automatic Hardware/Software Partitioning. In *Proceedings of MEMOCODE 2005*, pages 101–110. IEEE, 2005.

[KT04] Moez Krichen and Stavros Tripakis. Real-time testing with timed automata testers and coverage criteria. In *Joint conference on Formal Modelling and Analysis of Timed Systems and Formal Techniques in Real-Time and Fault Tolerant System (FORMATS-FTRTFT)*, LNCS 3253, pages 134–151. Springer, 2004.

[KTS+08] Christoph M. Kirchsteiger, Christoph Trummer, Christian Steger, Reinhold Weiss, and Markus Pistauer. *Distributed Embedded Systems: Design, Middleware and Resources*, chapter Specification-based Verification of Embedded Systems by Automated Test Case Generation, pages 35–44. Springer, 2008.

[Lee02] Edward A. Lee. Embedded software. *Advances in Computers*, 56:56–97, 2002.

[Lee03] Edward A. Lee. Overview of the Ptolemy Project. Technical report, EECS Department, University of California, Berkeley, Jul 2003.

[LMN05] Kim G. Larsen, Marius Mikucionis, and Brian Nielsen. *Formal Approaches to Software Testing*, chapter Online Testing of Real-time Systems Using UPPAAL, pages 79–94. Springer, 2005.

[Man05] Ka Lok Man. An Overview of SystemCFL. In *Research in Micro-*

electronics and Electronics, volume 1, pages 145–148, 2005.

[MFM+07] Ka Lok Man, Andrea Fedeli, Michele Mercaldi, Menouer Boubekeur, and Michel P. Schellekens. SC2SCFL: Automated SystemC to SystemCFL Translation. In *Embedded Computing Systems: Architectures, Modeling, and Simulation*, LNCS 4599, pages 34–45. Springer, 2007.

[MRR03] Wolfgang Müller, Jürgen Ruf, and Wolfgang Rosenstiel. *SystemC: Methodologies and Applications*, chapter An ASM based SystemC Simulation Semantics, pages 97–126. Kluwer Academic Publishers, 2003.

[NS01] Brian Nielsen and Arne Skou. Automated test generation from timed automata. In *Proceedings of the 7th International Conference on Tools and Algorithms for the Construction and Analysis of Systems (TACAS)*, LNCS 2031, pages 343–357. Springer, 2001.

[NZE+06] Amir Nahir, Avi Ziv, Roy Emek, Tal Keidar, and Nir Ronen. Scheduling-based test-case generation for verification of multimedia SoCs. In *DAC '06: Proceedings of the 43rd annual conference on Design automation*, pages 348–351, New York, NY, USA, 2006. ACM Press.

[Par08] Terence Parr. *ANTLR – ANother Tool for Language Recognition*. University of San Francisco, 2008. http://www.antlr.org.

[PP92] Shiv Prakash and Alice C. Parker. SOS: Synthesis of Application-Specific Heterogeneous Multiprocessor Systems. *Parallel and Distributed Computing*, 16:338–351, 1992.

[PS08] Hiren D. Patel and Sandeep K. Shukla. Model-driven validation of SystemC designs. *EURASIP Journal on Embedded Systems*, 2008(3):1–14, 2008.

[RHaR01] Jürgen Ruf, Dirk W. Hoffmann, and Thomas Kropf andWolfgang Rosenstiel. Simulation-guided property checking based on a multi-valued AR-automata. In *DATE '01: Proceedings of the conference on Design, automation and test in Europe*, pages 742–748, Piscataway, NJ, USA, 2001. IEEE Press.

[RHG+01] Jürgen Ruf, Dirk W. Hoffmann, Joachim Gerlach, Thomas Kropf andWolfgang Rosenstiel, and Wolfgang Müller. The Simulation Semantics of SystemC. In *Design, Automation and Test in Europe*, pages 64–70. IEEE Press, 2001.

[RMHL06] Christopher Robinson-Mallett, Robert M. Hierons, and Peter Liggesmeyer. Achieving communication coverage in testing. *ACM SIGSOFT Software Engineering Notes*, 31(6):1–10, 2006.

[Sal03]   Ashraf Salem. Formal Semantics of Synchronous SystemC. In *Design, Automation and Test in Europe (DATE)*, pages 10376–10381. IEEE Computer Society, 2003.

[SCV]   SystemC Verification Working Group SCV. SystemC Verification Standard. http://www.systemc.org.

[ST08]   Julien Schmaltz and Jan Tretmans. On conformance testing for timed systems. In *Formal Modeling and Analysis of Timed Systems (FORMATS)*, volume 5215 of *LNCS*, pages 250–264. Springer, 2008.

[SVD01]   Jan Springintveld, Frits Vaandrager, and Pedro R. D'Argenio. Testing timed automata. *Theoretical Computer Science*, 254(1–2):225–257, 2001.

[TCMM07] Claus Traulsen, Jerome Cornet, Matthieu Moy, and Florence Maraninchi:. A SystemC/TLM semantics in Promela and its possible applications. In *14th Workshop on Model Checking Software (SPIN '07)*, LNCS 4595, pages 204–222, Berlin, 2007. Springer.

[Tre96]   Jan Tretmans. Test generation with inputs, outputs and repetitive quiescence. *Software - Concepts and Tools*, 17(3):103–120, 1996.

[Tre08]   Jan Tretmans. Model based testing with labelled transition systems. In *Formal Methods and Testing*, volume 4949 of *LNCS*, pages 1–38. Springer, 2008.

[ZVM07]   Yu Zhang, Franck Vedrine, and Bruno Monsuez. SystemC Waiting-State Automata. In *First International Workshop on Verification and Evaluation of Computer and Communication Systems (VECoS 2007)*, 2007.

Supervised Diploma Theses

[Fel08]   Joachim Fellmuth. Automatische Übersetzung von SystemC Modellen in Timed Automata. Diploma Thesis, Technical University of Berlin, Software Engineering for Embedded Systems Group, June 2008.

[Fri09]   Florian Friedemann. Entwicklung eines Testorakels für die automatisierte Prüfung nichtdeterministischer Echtzeitsysteme. Diploma Thesis, Technical University of Berlin, Software Engineering for Embedded Systems Group, March 2009.

[Poc09]   Marcel Pockrandt. Optimierte Generierung von Konformitätstests für eingebettete Echtzeitsysteme. Diploma Thesis, Technical University of Berlin, Software Engineering for Embedded Systems Group, November 2009.